visiting **Frost**

visiting
Frost

Poems Inspired by the Life &

Work of ROBERT FROST

edited by SHEILA COGHILL

& THOM TAMMARO

Foreword by Jay Parini

UNIVERSITY OF IOWA PRESS *Iowa City*

University of Iowa Press, Iowa City 52242

Copyright © 2005 by the University of Iowa Press

Printed in the United States of America

Design by Richard Hendel

http://www.uiowa.edu/uiowapress

The University of Iowa Press is a member of Green Press
Initiative and is committed to preserving natural resources.

Printed on acid-free paper

Library of Congress Cataloging-in-Publication Data
Visiting Frost: poems inspired by the life and work of Robert Frost /
edited by Sheila Coghill and Thom Tammaro; foreword by Jay Parini.
p.   cm.
Includes index.
ISBN 0-87745-962-2 (cloth), ISBN 0-87745-963-0 (pbk.)
1. Frost, Robert, 1874–1963—Poetry.   2. Frost, Robert, 1874–1963—
Parodies, imitations, etc.   3. New England—Poetry.   4. Poets—Poetry.
5. American Poetry.   I. Coghill, Sheila, 1952–.   II. Tammaro, Thom.
PS3511.R94Z977 2005
811'.52—dc22   2005041762

05 06 07 08 09 C 5 4 3 2 1
05 06 07 08 09 P 5 4 3 2 1

There is a singer everyone has heard...

— ROBERT FROST, "The Oven Bird"

CONTENTS

Stealing from Frost

JAY PARINI

I've been reading the poems in this remarkable anthology with pleasure for the past month or so, freshly struck by the force of Robert Frost as an influence on modern and contemporary poets. His voice permeates American poetry. Frost remains a touchstone for many — if not most — poets who come after him. That so many interesting and strong poets have reached back into his work self-consciously and audaciously is the interesting news delivered by this book, and this news is likely to inspire and entertain a wide range of readers.

Writing is always a form of rewriting, of course. Poets rewrite their own words, but they also rewrite the words of other poets. Poetry is, in fact, a form of conversation, a way of talking with earlier poets and their poems. A great poet like Frost can be thought of as a kind of power station, one who stands off by himself in the big woods, continuously generating electricity that future poets can tap into for the price of a volume of his poems.

Some of the poets included here were contemporaries. (Indeed, Edward Thomas was among the poet's closest friends.) Richard Eberhart was not a close friend but met Frost on many occasions and learned a great deal from these encounters. In "Worldly Failure," he writes with some poignancy:

> I looked into the eyes of Robert Frost
> Once, and they were unnaturally deep.
> Set far back in the skull, as far back in the earth.
> An oblique glance made them look even deeper.

Eberhart, who lived in Cambridge for a period, was visiting his neighbor, Frost, at his house on Brewster Street. "He became a metaphor for inner devastation," Eberhart writes. In saying this, he would seem to be reading into the man what he had read in the poems. Eberhart knew of the hurt at the heart of that work, and he understood that much of the darkness in those poems — "Desert Places," "Aquainted with the Night," "Design" — grew from dark places in the poet's soul.

Many of the poems in this volume were written by an older generation of writers who had the good fortune to know Frost personally. Among those included here are Edward Thomas, Robert Francis, Robert Lowell, Howard Nemerov, Hayden Carruth, F. D. Reeve, William Meredith, Peter Davison, Theodore Weiss, Muriel Rukeyser, and Richard Wilbur. Their poems are, apart from anything else, memoirs as well as inventions, and they provide a valuable record of traces that Frost made on the world, in the minds of those who met him. For the most part, however, the poets writing here (like me) only came to know the man through the poems themselves, that amazing body of work.

Sometimes the poets included in this anthology respond to specific poems, as when Robert Cooperman reacts to "Good-by and Keep Cold." In a similar vein, Davi Walders revisits "Provide, Provide" in "The Kindness of Abishag," appropriating many of the rhythms of that poem in rather ingenious ways. Sometimes, as in Peter Meinke's "Robert Frost in Warsaw," the poet merely reflects on an image in a Frost poem, one that rises in the mind in a strange place:

When I saw birches in Wasienki Park
leaning against the wind, I thought of you,
old ghost, so strongly have you claimed those trees
for us.

Indeed, Frost claimed a certain landscape for himself, that region referred to in his work as being "north of Boston," with its birches and snowy fields, its dark woods and diverging paths, its icy mountain ponds, its apple orchards, stone walls, and horse-drawn sleighs. But he also claimed an anthology of moods, and these poems also reflect those moods, deepening or shifting them, reinventing them in unlikely and unexpected ways.

One of Frost's great rivals, T. S. Eliot, famously remarked that weak poets imitated earlier poets, while good poets simply stole from them. This was a provocative way of saying that a poet can take anything he or she needs to make a poem, as long as the "stealing" reinvents the passage, the line, the image, putting the earlier work into a fresh context. So many of the poets in this rich and varied collection do just that, as in X. J. Kennedy's memorable reinvention of "The Road Not Taken" or Mary Jo Salter's brilliant re-envisioning of Frost through the prism of Samuel Taylor Coleridge in her punning "Frost at Midnight."

Needless to say, poets pay homage to their forebears by arguing with them, as Michael S. Glaser does in "Quarreling with Robert Frost," a lively and feisty poem. But these quarrels are all (to appropriate Frost's wonderful phrase) lover's quarrels with the poet and his work.

Frost loomed large in his lifetime, casting a long shadow over American and English poetry. But that "shadow" need not be seen in any negative way. I'm always surprised, even stunned, by the power of that shade, by its ablity to not occlude the writers who choose to stand inside its penumbra. I'm surprised by the power of that shadow to change colors, to deepen and amplify the voice of the current speaker.

There is a singer everyone has heard, and that singer is Robert Frost. He had a lovely, strong, passionate, idiosyncratic, violent, sharp, deep, whimsical, witty, and wise voice. The reality presented by this anthology is that many gifted poets have listened to his songs, and they have found the tunes marvelous, and they have chosen to respond to those airs in their own measure, in their own strong voices. In this, there is cause for celebration.

Matter-of-Fact Magnificence

SHEILA COGHILL & THOM TAMMARO

As we did in *Visiting Emily* and *Visiting Walt*, we are, once again, in *Visiting Frost*, interested in listening to the conversations between contemporary poets and the poets who loom largest on the landscape of American poetry. Like Emily Dickinson and Walt Whitman, Robert Frost stands in that land- scape, straddling the nineteenth and twentieth centuries like a poetic colos- sus: whosoever desires passage must, at some point, contend with the monolithic presence of Robert Frost. Frost's life was filled with complexities and contradictions, an intricate, unfathomable web of emotional, intellec- tual, social, and familial tangles — all of this, of course, amplified by his being a public persona and, perhaps, the most recognizable literary figure in American literary history. No other poet in the history of this country had enjoyed the honor, recognition, and iconic public stature that Frost enjoyed by the time he stepped onto J.F.K.'s inaugural podium at about 11:00 A.M. on January 20, 1961. When it was suggested to him that Frost read at the inau- gural ceremony, even J.F.K. was aware of Frost's presence, replying, "Oh no! You know Frost always steals any show he is a part of!" Frost wrote that "the most satisfying part is to write a poem. The next most satisfying is to have people read them ... and to see poems turn up in quotations, become part of people's lives. Maybe turn up in a Presidential campaign." We know that there would have been no Maya Angelou or Miller Williams at Bill Clinton's side and no James Dickey at Jimmy Carter's inaugural celebration if there had been no Robert Frost standing at J.F.K.'s side in the glinting late morning sunlight.

Ask a stranger on the street to name an American poet, and Frost's name will surely be uttered more often than not. We recognize Frost's poems as inextricable threads in the educational fabric of this country. Is there anyone in this nation who has not read or memorized a Frost poem during his or her school years? For many, Frost's poetic presence may be the only poetic pres- ence felt — or at least remembered — in their lives; his voice, the only one resonating in their ears, for the rest of their lives. But oh, what a voice it is! Frost continues to be the great poetic presence in the lives and work of our own poets, as well as in the lives of millions of other Americans who do not read or write poetry.

Our contending views of Robert Frost are captured shortly after his death in Robert Lowell's 1963 tribute to Frost in the *New York Review of Books*: "I have heard him say mockingly that hell was a half-filled auditorium. This was a hell he never had to suffer. Year after year after year, he was as great a drawing-card as Dylan Thomas was in his brief prime. Yet there was a strain; never in his life was he able to eat before a reading. A mutual friend of ours once said with pity, 'It's sad to see Frost storming about the country when he might have been an honest schoolteacher.'"

With measured cadences solidified by classical harmonies of sound made accessible through an identifiable landscape and common language, Frost mends our sense of fragmentation in the modern world. His poetry pleases our ear with what Randall Jarrell called its "matter-of-fact magnificence." Frost himself defined a poem as "a momentary stay against confusion" and as an artistic medium reflecting stability and permanence invoked by the moment of the poem.

The early part of the twentieth century is commonly thought of in terms of its revolution in *vers libre*; others think of it in terms of the abandonment of form. And while many poets took up Whitman's sweeping open form and tried, with Pound, to "make it new," Frost followed a clearly formed path that had never been abandoned, just less favored in the fast-paced world of pre- and postwar America as the shock of the new settled in. As Annie Finch has observed in *The Ghost of Meter*, "Non-metrical verse was as common in American poetry during the beginning of the twentieth century as iambic pentameter had been in English and American poetry for the preceding three hundred and fifty years."

In this "re-discovered" tradition of metered form, Frost crafted what he loved best, namely, the paradoxes of pleasure and "worriment." In this vein, this anthology presents one hundred poems inspired by Frost's pastoral renditions of nature, the bleakness of moments of human suffering, the dramatic melodramas of family and marriage, the darkness of imponderable dilemmas, the whimsy of wry amusements in the world's enthusiasms, and singular acerbic observations about human follies. All of this Frost derived from life. In his biography *Robert Frost: A Life*, Jay Parini aptly articulates these distilled paradoxes about Frost:

> The contradictions of his life and work remain stunning. He was a loner who liked company; a poet of isolation who sought a mass audience; a rebel who sought to fit in. Although a family man to the core, he frequently felt alienated from his wife and children and withdrew into reveries. While preferring to stay at home, he traveled more than any poet of his generation to give lectures and readings, even though he remained terrified of public speaking. . . . He was a democrat who hated Franklin Roosevelt, a poet of labor who could not support the New Deal. He believed passionately in war as a rational and justifiable response to certain international crises, yet he could not stir in himself much interest in the Second World War. He was an ardent supporter of Eisenhower in 1960 — and who publicly identified himself with Kennedy by reading at his inauguration. He was a fierce anti-communist who embraced Nikita Khrushchev personally, calling him "a great man."

We hope the poems in *Visiting Frost* honor these contradictions, which Frost himself managed to surmount and blend to perfection. Frost wanted to preserve his most common poetic subjects — the fading New England country life and dialect, rural landscapes and history — by fixing them indelibly in an immortal poetry, for he always retained something of the notions his mother taught him as a child: a creative act is one inspired by God, the impulse to write is divine, and poetry could express dimensions of immortality.

Yet, if there is one truth to be gleaned in the complexity of Frost's life, certainly it is his steadfast commitment and dedication to a life of poetry. Frost's vision of where poetry should be in our personal and collective lives was always clear: he believed it should be at the center. Certainly, it was at the center of his life. His biographers make this clear. Read Frost's 1930 address to the Amherst Alumni Council, "Education by Poetry," and you will understand his passions. And, of course, as if to deliver poetry to the people and country himself, there was Frost, beginning in 1916 and continuing to his death in 1963, crisscrossing the country, teaching seminars and lecturing at dozens of universities and colleges (he visited one college nineteen times!), and giving public talks and reading his poems to tens of thousands of people. He often returned home from these reading and lecture tours ill and exhausted. Even late in his life — in fact, less than six months before his death — Frost, eighty-eight, at the invitation of President Kennedy, traveled to Russia as part of a cultural exchange program sponsored by the State Department. There, he engaged in a series of nonstop State Department engagements, readings, and meetings with Russian writers and intellectuals, culminating in his meeting at a resort on the Black Sea with Khrushchev, who had to go to Frost's guest house to meet him because Frost was ill and exhausted from his Russian itinerary. If poetry failed to lodge itself in this nation's heart and soul, it certainly was not because of Frost's failings.

Inspired by these distilled mixtures of fluidity and permanence, many contemporary poets capture the refracted images of Frost, the man and his work. William Olsen expresses this in "Frost's Last Lecture: A Tape: His Audience — 1963":

> They are listening to what he hears. They are long ago.
> They step into the lecture, it's never the same twice.
>
> . . .
>
> they are listening to what they heard and what he heard.
> He seems too lost in his notes to go the rest of the way.
>
> . . .
>
> sometimes it's remorse, sometimes it's nearly hope,
> sometimes it's something they couldn't bear to hope.

This "listening" has both literal and figurative dimensions. A whole generation recalls, as does Lex Runciman: ". . . one day, / January, [Frost] standing / in the black box of our television, / holding a paper / suddenly gone white / and silent in cold sun. / So he put it down / and began reciting / 'The Gift Outright'. . ."

This touchstone image imparts for today's generations of writers an indelible moment in memory and prosody. This memory is more than just an impression. It is carried by what Samuel Maio, in an essay in the *Formalist*, depicts as Frost's belief "that everyday conversation could be used to carry traditional poetic forms (iambic meter, rhyming patterns, form and style:

sonnets, odes, elegies)." This is part of Frost's poetic genius, to marry form so that it deftly presents its topic but makes the structure invisible yet strong enough to convey sincerity of voice, occasional apparent self-revelation, and gentle self-deprecation while employing the most intricate and delicate stanza forms. This craftsmanship is captured in Hayden Carruth's "The Woodcut on the Cover of Robert Frost's *Complete Poems*."

Recalling the languor of Keats (to whose poetry Frost acknowledged indebtedness) Frost writes in a 1914 letter to Robert Bridges: "The living part of a poem is the intonation entangled somehow in the syntax, idiom and meaning of a sentence. It is only here for those who have heard it previously in conversation. . . . It is the most volatile and at the same time important part of poetry." Those who have "heard it previously in conversation" include the speaker in Marvin Bell's "Unable to Sleep in Frost's Bed in Franconia," who "has listened hard to the voices / that blur the vision of one's time," and the speaker in Kim Bridgford's "Robert Frost": "You seemed to be the voice that spoke the poems: / Genial, meandering . . ." Peter Davison hears it, too, in "Getting over Robert Frost": "All those evenings cradled in the sway / of the old man's gnarled hands / . . . Such an influence seeps in and stays. / I am thankful / for his friendship." And so does Dave Mason, recalling sitting in a car with his father and hearing of Frost's death, then two weeks later of Sylvia Plath's death, in "Winter, 1963." And so does Galway Kinnell in "For Robert Frost": "Why do you talk so much / Robert Frost? . . . Is it that talk / Doesn't have to be metered and rhymed? / Or is talk distracting from something worse?" In Frost, we discover "conversations" which hold promises that can be kept because they are assured by the familiar movement of his syntax while also promising "adventure."

We hope that readers of this anthology will enter these conversations, and that the poems herein echo the "sound of sense" that Frost loved so much. We hope it also offers readers the "understanding" of poetry. In an interview with Harvey Breit of the *New York Times*, Frost expresses this too: "If poetry isn't understanding all, the whole world, then it isn't worth anything. Young poets forget that poetry must include the mind as well as the emotions. Too many poets delude themselves by thinking the mind is dangerous and must be left out. Well, the mind is dangerous and must be left in." The poets and poems in this anthology have not left out anything. They have given us finely crafted and thoughtful work. The surfaces seem smooth yet give us complexities within.

Frost gave to Americans what he gave to Nobel Prize poet Seamus Heaney. In his 1995 Nobel lecture "Crediting Poetry," Heaney said: "To begin with, I wanted that truth to life to possess a concrete reliability, and rejoiced most when the poem seemed most direct, an upfront representation of the world it stood in for or stood up for or stood its ground against. Even as a schoolboy . . . I loved Robert Frost for his farmer's accuracy and his wily down-to-earthness." Elsewhere, Heaney has written that "Frost corroborated a part of me that needed to know that the world of a County Derry farm could be given a look-in in English blank verse. But, of course, this documentary aspect of his work was only one part of his attraction, because you read Frost as much for his melody as for his subject matter. You read him because of the way the very realistic narratives and dialogues came off the page and right into the ear." Frost wove his American stories and talk into blank verse melodies as fine as any ever written in the history of American verse.

In his introduction to *King Jasper*, the 1935 posthumous collection of poems by E. A. Robinson, Frost wrote: "The utmost ambition is to lodge a few poems where they will be hard to get rid of, to lodge a few irreducible bits." "After Apple-Picking," "Birches," "Choose Something Like a Star," "The Death of the Hired Man," "Design," "Directive," "Dust of Snow," "Fire and Ice," "The Gift Outright," "Home Burial," "Mending Wall," "Mowing," "Nothing Gold Can Stay," "Out, Out —," "The Pasture," "A Patch of Old Snow," "Provide, Provide," "The Road Not Taken," "Stopping by Woods on a Snowy Evening," "The Tuft of Flowers." Will those suffice for your share, Mr. Frost? Have those lodged deep enough for you, Mr. Frost?

Try as we may, it is still impossible to measure Frost's full influence and shape in the contours of American poetry. We must be satisfied with running our fingers along the smooth, melodious fabric of his poems and feeling his presence. We hope this anthology will suggest just how alive and vital Frost remains more than forty years after his death and in the early years of the new millennium — we hope to suggest just how much Frost's words matter. Feeling the contour of his life and work in the poems that follow will be homage and testimony to his enduring presence.

As the poets in this anthology demonstrate, they have "heard" Frost's "voice." As Jay Parini points out in his biography, "Frost himself cautioned against finding in his poems irrelevant ambiguities, with connotations spreading like ink on blotting paper. Metaphors and symbols provide a way of delimiting (as well as opening out) meaning; thus, the poet controls the reading of a poem, sharply defining its boundaries. No one understood that better than Frost." As this collection of poems illustrates, the range of well-crafted poetry gives us the delights of directed chance, the adventure of both mind and imagination, and a tribute to Frost's own "matter-of-fact magnificence."

■

As editors, we take full responsibility for any errors in the collection. Every effort will be made to correct any errors we discover — as well as those brought to our attention by readers — in future printings or editions. As with all such projects, there are many people to thank. We would like to begin by thanking the many writers here for their generosity, support, enthusiasm, and patience with us during the editing process. We also would like to thank the many editors and publishers who helped arrange permissions to reprint many of these poems. For their special interest in the anthology and their assistance, a special thanks to David Lehman; Kim Stafford and Paul Merchant at the William Stafford Archives; Lorna Scott, senior information adviser at the University of Gloucestershire; Colin G. Thornton, Honorable Secretary, the Edward Thomas Fellowship; Anne Harvey, editor of *Elected Friends*; and Roland Dille, president emeritus, Minnesota State University Moorhead. We are especially grateful to Jay Parini for taking time from his busy schedule of writing, editing, and teaching to write the foreword and for offering his poem. Again, we are grateful to Holly Carver, director of the University of Iowa Press, and to her small but enormously talented staff for their enthusiasm, professionalism, attention, and support throughout this project. We continue to be impressed by the number of books — and by their striking quality and design — that the Kuhl House crew is capable of producing in any given year.

We would also like to thank our many friends and colleagues at Minnesota State University Moorhead for their support and assistance:

Shelly Heng, Dee Kruger, and David Leukam for help with preparing the manuscript; Angela Jones, teaching assistant and friend, for her editorial assistance; Stacey Voeller, electronic resources librarian, and Dianne Schmidt, library technician in the Interlibrary Loan Department, for their patience with us and for their help in tracking down numerous poems and rare and out-of-print books in a timely manner; and Bette Midgarden, vice president for academic affairs, for her continued support. We would like to thank Minnesota State University Moorhead for its support in the forms of a Faculty Development Grant and a sabbatical leave, during which much of the work for this anthology was completed.

Stay Home

WENDELL BERRY

I will wait here in the fields
to see how well the rain
brings on the grass.
In the labor of the fields
longer than a man's life
I am at home. Don't come with me.
You stay home too.

I will be standing in the woods
where the old trees
move only with the wind
and then with gravity.
In the stillness of the trees
I am at home. Don't come with me.
You stay home too.

visiting **Frost**

A Second-Grade Incident from Robert Frost's Childhood

JOE AIMONE

One day of kindergarten had scared
The poet off. He'd learned at home
Thereafter, till now, trying again,
Believing that he needn't go.

No discipline ever appealed
To him but voluntary love,
Which is a trifle wild, it seems,
But will not easily give up.

See him there with his hands outstretched
For slapping, his face dark with crime,
Who crawled down rows behind the desks
To steal an extra Valentine.

Trying to Sleep on My Father's Couch and Staring at the Fractured Plaster, I Recall

TONY BARNSTONE

some poem with girls on hands and knees, but now
it seems I can't remember anything.
The words inside my mind have turned to snow,
though lines emerge like trees a boy could swing
on, climbing to the top until the tree
can bear no more but dips its head
and sets him down again. I think I see
them now, those sexy girls with long hair spread
before them drying on the ground, while up
the stiff tall trees the boy keeps climbing till
they bend down limp and spent. Can't seem to fall
asleep. Instead I climb with mixed-up lust
through memory. (Think snow. Lie still.) But still
I climb the cracks and shadows up the wall.

Late December, Where Are You, Robert Frost?

WILLIS BARNSTONE

Where are you, Robert Frost? The first poems
I heard were yours which you recited on
the stages of my many schools. "Rough gems"
my teachers called them and called you "the con
man of the cracker barrel." Jealous snobs.
Plato wrote for the tomb of his ally,
Tyrant of Syracuse, "Honored by the mobs
of patriots — but I was one who loved you, my
friend Dion!" Once in Middletown, we three,
Snow, Frost and Stone sat down to eat a cold
lunch. Almost deaf you did the talking, told
how you read Homer only in the Greek
at Harvard, quit and hit the woods. I see
your face this morning, fresh, and winter bleak.

Unable to Sleep in Frost's Bed in Franconia

MARVIN BELL

The floor shone from nightmare.
It made little difference which path I took
chasing oblivion — mind's eye or the avenue out.
He too walked for hours just to meet up
with midnight. Who walks these long nights
has seen in the moon the cragged face of a farmer
lighting the withered crops that live but
a short season. And by rock walls that rose only
to clear a field, has listened hard to the voices
that blur the vision of one's time:
smear of tree sap and the juice of crushed fruit,
blood from the fly and the gorged spider. Thus it was
that I lay expecting something of the old man's
genealogy. I heard a cracking wise
in the floorboards, or so I thought, as I looked for sleep.
It was chilly. I had only a light blanket
which I pulled over my head to hold my breath in.

Frost and His Enemies

ROBERT BLY

When Robert Frost set down a poetic whim,
The darkness with open mouth went looking for him.

Flowers love sun; but larvae, even at noon,
In their murky pond are excited by the moon!

When a foot in a marsh works to get free,
Water fills up the hole immediately.

When Frost sat down to get a poem right,
He was a sandy place open to night.

He wanted to see white, even if it were a birch,
Or a patch of snow or the steeple of a church.

After Snow-Mobiling

ALEC BOND

My sleek, streamlined machine's lying in a drift
Pointed at Ely still,
And there's a shrub I didn't kill
Beside it, and there may be someone miffed
Because I chased his cow.
But I am done with snow-mobiling now.
The scent of spring is heavy in the air,
Fresh from the pig-parlors; and I'm flaked out.
I can hardly rub the grease out of my hair
Got from taking carburetors apart
This morning when I shifted a pair
To my friend's new Arctic Cat:
I barely knew where I was at
When I got home to catch some sleep,
And I could see my dreams didn't stand a prayer
Of being anything but deep.
Low-lying clotheslines, an attacking buck,
Antlers pointed at my chin,
And a wood-tick close enough to pluck —
They made me feel a perfect has-been.
I felt the leather seat bend with my weight,
And I kept hearing from the back stretch
The rumbling low
Of car after car of bikers come to fetch
Me home, as we drove through the falling snow.
For I have had too much
Of snow-mobiling: I am overweary
Of the great race I ran myself, dearie,
Of putting down and letting out the clutch
And shifting gears mile after mile.
Don't smile

At those hair-pin turns
On which I almost rolled my rig
Or at the friction burns
On hand or leg.
A turn missed was a race lost —
Even, as though I hadn't made the run.
You can see what will bother
This snooze of mine, if I get one.
Had she not stampeded farther
The cow might say, for fun,
If it's like chewing fodder
Or more like Copenhagen.

Elinor White Frost Speaks

N. M. BREWKA

I didn't think there was room in the world for yet
another poet, which is why I took the leather pamphlet
you handed me through a door I didn't even wish to open,
thumbed through, and turned away from you.

I couldn't think of a use in the world for a man who wrote
about butterflies, not unless he was dissecting one to
contribute to science. I had thought you smarter than that,
Dartmouth-bound with your bread family-buttered.

New Hampshire, Massachusetts, Vermont,
all cold places, that's what I learned from you,
all about cold places, England, too. Even in August,
the unmowed hay looked like drifting snow.

My politics: I ate off your words, hating my own
handouts. I had been entitled once, to be read like an
open book, but somewhere along the line, I shut
that trap. My duty was to love you cover to cover.

Robert Frost

KIM BRIDGFORD

You seemed to know the most about the dark,
But softened it, so we would listen, still
As leaves before they show they're vulnerable
To wind. You seemed to know the grief of work,
And also joy, depending on the weather
And how the critics saw your poems. You seemed
To know how tragedy could happen, aimed
At no one, but simple as a signature.

You seemed to be the voice that spoke the poems:
Genial, meandering, New England to the core.
And yet you never were; you played the part.
The mask you wore enabled the extremes:
The truth that fingers ice and whispers fire.
It was the neighbor's voice that made it art.

Of Robert Frost

GWENDOLYN BROOKS

There is a little lightning in his eyes.
Iron at the mouth.
His brows ride neither too far up nor down.

He is splendid. With a place to stand.

Some glowing in the common blood.
Some specialness within.

The Woodcut on the Cover of Robert Frost's *Complete Poems*

HAYDEN CARRUTH

For Wendell Berry

A man plowing starts at the side of the field
Nearer home and works outward and away.
Why? Because plowing is always an adventure.
Then walking home with the horses at end of day.

Poem Beginning with a Line from Frost

DAN CHIASSON

as if regret were in it and were sacred
    as if regret itself were a river and want

which was the source of that river flowed
    through the river, more and more the more

the river thickened towards the boring lake
    where what stirred once went terribly quiet.

This is indistinguishable from happiness.
    This standing water was a mindful current once.

Once was a mindful current: now leaden, still:
    it is ourselves we most resemble now; now

the maples that had been nowhere gather. When
    we look down we look down on our own.

The Ghosts of Luxury

BRUCE COHEN

Sometime in the '50s, Robert Frost, a visiting
professor at Berkeley, desired, Frost desired
to meet baseball players & was introduced
to a curly haired cherubic blond who later
became Rookie of the Year for the Bosox:
Jackie Jensen. They talked into the espresso
evenings mostly baseball but a little poetry too,

& stayed periodic New England pals.
Jackie often left tickets for Mr. Frost.
I'm embarrassed by my love for this story,
void of drama, its only point, the oddness of friends.
July 1993: my first Fenway visit. The Green Monster.
Steel girders obstruct some of the cheap seats.
A man's value is measured by his seat at a baseball game.

I thought of my father, how he'd be a little proud —
me, in the sky box with free beer & unlimited franks.
The dead don't need to know the why of anything.
He'd just brag to his scalper cronies in heaven.
No doubt he'd think I've become something, but what
would he ask besides the names of my sons?
If I'm happy? I once swore I'd never

mention happiness in a poem, so I'd just nod.
I know loss & luxury began in 1961 because the National
League didn't exist, did not exist in New York.
I know it was 1961 because the city was buzzing
Mantle & Maris & 61 Jacks, the city pregnant
with Mets. Upon their birth in '62 my father
no longer needed to wake me at 4 A.M.

No, nothing was wrong. He simply needed
to drive to Philly to catch the Giants: the closest
they'd get to New York for a year. (Save the World Series.)
In 1961, in the House That Ruth Built, my father thought
out loud, look at those slobs in the bleachers.
If every one gave us a buck, no one would miss it,
or even think twice, & baby, we'd be fucking rich.

As time erodes, one's definition of luxury changes.
Any moron can identify the wealthy. Seasons
are so casual, so insignificant, they treat them as verbs.
(We summered along the Seine.) At Fenway my buddies
& I waited till everyone but the sweepers left the stadium,
then snuck onto the darkened field. Fred pretended to bat.
I threw an imaginary curve from the pitcher's rubber.

I believe I saw the ghost of Robert Frost in the bleachers —
Jackie Jensen in the dugout thumbing the complete
poems of the Queen of Amherst, & my old man,
wolfing a hot dog in three bites, a cigarette glowing
in his other hand. My definition of luxury is constant,
a baseball game, the way you plan nothing after
cause there's no telling how long it'll last,

the play not restricted by time, but by the number
of failures, (outs), a sport that invades all four seasons.
Luxury *has* changed. When I have a late work
meeting & not enough time to go home and come back,
I hoard the hour at a Chinese restaurant,
not thinking about my wife, my boys,
the third kicking her belly. After the meal,

the waitress formally announces: a fortune cookie.
I crumble it & find a lucky mistake:
three fortunes. I forget the first two.
The last said He who has imagination
without the darkening has wings but no feet.
But even that may not be right ...
If not for failures, nothing would ever end.

Postcard from Robert Frost's Grave

WYN COOPER

Amy was crooning and Linda was swooning the night I brought them here. Her baritone led us in Irish songs of mourning, liquid as the Guinness which helped us sing. Linda asked that we show respect, but the director relieved himself behind two birches that grow near the grave. Amy sang the blues, her voice so low only the ground could hear. We were louder than fireworks on the Fourth of July, which we watched from the End of the World. We sang along with Amy as Linda rubbed the stone. The northern lights lit up our thoughts, but cops arrived to shut us up. A lover's quarrel with the world indeed.

Good-by and Keep Cold

ROBERT COOPERMAN

Keep cold, young orchard. Good-by and keep cold.
Dread fifty above more than fifty below.
— Robert Frost

Frost meant fruit trees and their need
to avoid the summer's bark-peeling heat,
but I can remember someone I wanted
to say "Good-by and keep cold" to,
not meant as a kindness either.
Sad to think how love or its likeness
spends itself, dries up, withers,
burns and turns to ashes that stick
grittily to the tongue, to the mind
for years until all that's left
is the memory of a last encounter,
a final combat of wills, a bitterness
as of something charred in a recipe
followed not too exactly:

A memory of standing at a bus stop
after it was all over and seeing her
suddenly emerge from a store
and feeling nothing except a curse
that never got uttered,
a sneer never curving onto my lips
as she strode past and tried
to pretend I wasn't there,
her eyes saying, "Get off this piece
of sidewalk you've ruined for me,"
mine answering, "Freeze to death."

Then she was gone, and the day
in shards for the both of us,
wind slapping my face, my only
spiteful comfort to think
it was causing tears to form
in her eyes, the sudden drop
in temperature making them turn
cold and hard as iron
I wished my heart was made of.

Grandmother Living in Fear of Free Verse

NINA CORWIN

In the nightmare scenarios of a Jewish grandmother
      the free verse granddaughter
is discovered unconscious and unscrubbed
              in some grungy neon-lit hotel
wearing underwear
      that hasn't been washed in over a week

or living a life of wild, out-of-wedlock sex
          with uncircumcised men
    of third world descent
              and derelict days
spent rummaging through dusty ashtrays
      for a toke on the butt of a stubbed out inspiration.

          Do you want to end up
like that awful Ann Sexton, she demands,
    or Allen Ginsberg, *oy gevalt*,
      his poor mother,
so I tell her Ginsberg's mother was crazy
before he came along
    and maybe that's why he became a poet.

She shakes a volume of Robert Frost in my
face announcing *here*, in metered quatrains
and no uncertain terms, *is a real poet*
and by the way, don't quit your day job.

I wonder if she's read the last pages
      where he lapses
into an anarchy of unrhymed passages, the luxury
    of barefoot narrative falling just short
      of uneven lines,
the subversive pleasure
      of random: punctuation
      !

Building Walls

TODO DAVIS

Before I built a wall I'd ask to know
What I was walling in or walling out...
— Robert Frost

At the edge of our woods,
when the trees begin to green
and you say
       it is time to go for stone,
       the rocks begin to surface.

They grow large in surrounding fields,
backs of the baptized
cleaned by storms,
       and their weight, pushing toward blue,
       settles darkly.

In late afternoon we sweat
with the effort of moving stone from earth
while spring sun,
       still pushed to the far horizon,
       begins to take our working light.

Rusted wheelbarrow carries what will be today's last load,
and together, where our field ends and the world begins,
we touch,
       shoulder to shoulder,
       fitting stone upon stone.

Getting over Robert Frost

PETER DAVISON

All those evenings cradled in the sway
     of the old man's gnarled hands
          gently chopping the air

woke my nostrils to the fragrance of
     my mind, eased out
          the frequencies my ears could reach.

Such an influence seeps in and stays.
     I'm thankful
          for his friendship, as I'm indebted to my

genes — though it's taken years to comprehend
     that a great poet is only a great
          poet: neither a father nor a force

of generation. I was born entitled to
     the liberty of breathing easy, but I had to learn
          the trick of not trusting a line

unless it flickered with
     my own odor, the taste of
          myself. And then I got over him,

welcoming the little victories of
     waking up, learning that not all harmonies
          need to be prodded or bent

to take on tragic overtones, that
     music need not always express
          regret at having
          disappointed someone.

Still Life

MADELINE DEFREES

The question that he frames in all but words
Is what to make of a diminished thing.
— Robert Frost, "The Oven Bird"

After your letter arrived I left the oven on
all night and never once
put my head in it. After your letter arrived
I let one foot follow the other
through the better part of the day. Your letter
lay on the kitchen table by the paring
knife on the stoneware plate with the apple core
like a Dutch still life restored to
its muted color.

      In the sink a spiral of lemon
peel twisted like smoke toward the past and I
think that I let it lie.
The first day of night these eyes you opened
were glassed and dry as your late martini.
The next they brimmed into morning.
It was time to rehearse the Sunday phone call,
the new role laid out for learning.
When you asked,

      Did you get my letter? I picked up
the cue as if you had wired me
roses in winter or proposed
a pas de deux. Then partly for your sake I taught
myself to sing the best song I could make:
the burden of the oven bird's diminished thing. Sang
wash of sunlight on the sill and apple core,
sang water glass half full of emptiness. Sang body
all in shadow that I must bathe and dress.

Apparently Someone in the Department

GEORGE DREW

SUBJECT: A CERTAIN DEAD WHITE POET (MALE)

FROM: Vera Slattjam <slattjam@hvale.edu>

Apparently someone in the department
has assigned Robert Frost. If you,
would you let me know? For your sake,
and that of your students, I hope
it isn't "stopping by" those woods again,
isn't the usual milieu-driven mood
manipulation — the dark, the frozen lake,
snow falling, that man in his sled.
Why not radically reinvent the man
as a Calvinist with murder on his mind?
Maybe a laconic Vermonter, maybe you.
How about an allegory? In this scenario
what's murdered is the classics — known,
in prehistoric times, as the canon. Pound's
no problem, nor Hart Crane, nor Robinson,
Stevens, Cummings and others of his kind,
and certainly not Williams, nor Eliot —
Thomas Stearns, that is. But *Robert Frost*?
That granite-tongued bundle of testosterone?
How about someone somewhat more obscure?
Say J. V. Cunningham, or Weldon Kees?
Or someone British, far away from this?
George Darley, for example. Or John Clare,
who didn't know whose woods they were
and didn't care. Who plowed ahead,
no more constrained by promises than Faust.
Madness is a quite acceptable excuse,

but your syllabus is due today — revised.
Frost doesn't belong in Freshman English II.

                    Cheers,

                         Vera

Worldly Failure

RICHARD EBERHART

I looked into the eyes of Robert Frost
Once, and they were unnaturally deep.
Set far back in the skull, as far back in the earth.
An oblique glance made them look even deeper.

He stood inside the door on Brewster Street,
Looking out. I proffered him an invitation.
We went on talking for an hour and a half.
To accept or not to accept was his question,

Whether he wanted to meet another poet;
He erred in sensing some intangible slight.
Hard for him to make a democratic leap.
To be a natural poet you have to be unnaturally deep.

While he was talking he was looking out,
But stayed in, sagacity better indoors.
He became a metaphor for inner devastation,
Too scared to accept my invitation.

For Robert Frost

RHINA P. ESPAILLAT

Easy as breath, without a trace of toil,
your lines uncoil, roll off the spool you wound
so that to shift one syllable would spoil
the spin of image or the flow of sound.
I turn your poem inside-out to see
what sleight-of-hand disguised as accident
transmutes the music into tapestry
without the knots and errors of intent,

but find your words are really only words
like those we use, and do not give away
the spell that works you into them. So birds
juggle their ordinary scales to say
extraordinary things. Like them, you came
to make our songs no longer quite the same.

A Farm in the Green Mountains

DAVE ETTER

Thinking of Robert Frost

Stone upon stone
this weathered wall of stone
was built by men deviled by stone
from poor fields yielding mostly stone.

Stone upon stone
this Vermont wall of stone
was the sure employment of stone
in a place that is shaped by stone.

Stone upon stone
this ragged wall of stone
was a grudging tribute to stone
by farmers making peace with stone.

Night Call

ANNIE FINCH

I think of your quiet grave now and again
When innocence has rolled me out of sleep
And close to my man's side, to lean again
Against his breathing human side, to keep
Myself breathed in his liquid human breath.
I think of your nurturing grave so often. Death
Has made you a place I like to imagine going:
Opening the gate to your grave, entering in,
Reaping your silence, where the small tree, growing
Generous in the forgiveness of your sin,
Leans over your stone, the grass, your bones, the grass,
The grass. The grass. I like to imagine frost there, hung
Like frost on a beach in November, when the sun
Rises on winter, just as it rose on spring,
On the humid decision to grow, past everything.

Mrs. Post's 6th-Hour English Class

SUSAN FIRER

Milwaukee, 1966
Old, white-haired Mrs. Post slippered
her joined and curved 4 fingers into her every
dress' white-laced V-neck. There she

moved her hand metrically up &
down between her freckled breasts
the whole while she read to us.
That day it was Robert Frost.

Reading Frost, by any second
quatrain, Mrs. Post became transported.
Scansion increased her heartbeat.
Spondees visibly shortened her breath.

That hot afternoon we read
"Stopping by Woods on a Snowy
Evening" her recitation
even gave me a slight shiver.

It was summer. Wasps had flown
into our opened classroom windows.
Girls waved hand-folded theme-paper fans;
boys after lunch dozed. The class

had just left the snow-
filled woods on the "darkest evening of the year."
There "the little horse" near the frozen lake
was still shaking his harness bells, &
in the lonely dark the wind was still

blowing. Oh no, now the class was off
to a "yellow wood." Someone was sighing.
It wasn't me. I was lost. I could not keep up,
but I was happily lost in clicking

ice-covered birches, in "magnified apples," in
"domes of heaven." When I finally managed
to catch up, Mrs. Post was in philodendrons.
No, no she wasn't in philodendrons.
She was summing up

"The Road Not Taken": "Phil o soph i cal.
Verrry philosophical." And that was when
she posed the question: "What did Frost mean
'I took the one less traveled by
And that has made all the difference'?"

Now, here, I believe we are close to the moment
where I decide to be a poet. Debbie Siegel,
whose mother — and everyone knows this —
drove the family's mink-colored Impala
into the family's swimming pool
only a week before,

Debbie, who everyone knows never speaks
except in gym class or home economics,
raised her arm and
impatiently waved her hand
as if cleaning a stubborn streak off a window.

Possibly in anticipation of all
post-structural theory, Debbie said,
"It is clear
if the speaker of the poem had traveled
the more traveled road, he would
have ended up at the milkman's. Since
he did not need milk that day,
he took the road less traveled."

What?? Even, even
the most completely uninterested students
perked up then. What was happening?
Mrs. Post's hand flew out of her dress.

Michael Durkin sat up and started sputtering.
Susan O'Toole of the best jumpers and knee socks
was about to try logic. (LOGIC???
What does logic have to do with poetry?)
When the bell prizefight-loud rang,

we all returned to our corners, but, & this
is important: We were not untouched.
Judy Feenburg's black ponytail
whipped her cheeks from her agitated
head swinging as she exited.
And I, I believe, I was changed also.
I left Mrs. Post's room bedraggled
with words and their possibilities
to create hallucinations
          quiet breathing
to create bouquets of confusion
          & feasts of loss

and in Debbie Siegel's case that summer afternoon
to focus attention on syntax and grammar.
Never before in Mrs. Post's class,
or in any other class that I shared with her,
had Debbie ever spoken so well

with such precision, such elaborately
constructed and weirdly considered
comments, and I, for one, have always been
grateful to both Debbie and old, white-haired
Mrs. Post, who had the wisdom,
that afternoon, to allow us to leave her
classroom in such sweet suspension of sense,

which I grew to understand as
only one of the many glittered

costumes of the lively breath-
ful poems I am always
growing to love.

On a Theme by Frost

ROBERT FRANCIS

Amherst never had a witch
Of Coös or of Grafton

But once upon a time
There were three old women.

One wore a small beard
And carried a big umbrella.

One stood in the middle
Of the road hailing cars.

One drove an old cart
All over town collecting junk.

They were not weird sisters,
No relation to one another.

A duly accredited witch I
Never heard Amherst ever had

But as I say there
Were these three old women.

One was prone to appear
At the door (not mine!):

"I've got my nightgown on,
I can stay all night."

One went to a party
At the president's house once

Locked herself in the bathroom
And gave herself a bath.

One had taught Latin, having
Learned it at Mount Holyoke.

Of course Amherst may have
Had witches I never knew.

Indirective

JAMES GALVIN

The ridge road takes the ridgespine every way
It turns. It threads the granite vertebrae
And old, wind-dwarfed ponderosas that twist
Out of the ungiving, unforgiving ground
Like tips of auger bits drilled through from Hell.
Here, all trees die by lightning soon or late.
This hidden side-trail elk hunters found will fall
To their camp on Sheep Creek, where the creek stops them.
They ignite their Colemans, dress the carcasses,
Make drunk display in artificial light.
Years past the road kept going, forded there.
Now the creek has cut and caved the bank.
You have to go on horseback or afoot.
Well, just as well. Afoot or horseback was
The only way to go before the road,
Before the reason for the road arrived,
Disguised as some old trapper, moonshiner,
Xenophobe, or who the hell he was —
Old badger, anyway, who cleared some trees,
Cut some sidehill and creekbank with a slip
And mule to get a wagon way in there
With stores to keep him winterlong and when
The water rose too high to ford, Lord knows.
I said I'd take you there but I don't know.
More than likely I'll just get us lost.
The last time I tried to find the old homestead
I poked around for it awhile and then
Rode on to look for some of Richard's strays.
I never saw a cow that day either.
But I'll take you up and we can look
If your heart's set on it. The only time

I saw the place myself I was with Ray.
Well, now Ray's dead, but he knew where it was,
Back then you could still drive there four-wheel-drive,
Before the crossing disappeared. Even
Then the bank was steep for Ray's old Scout.
We lost the clutch, but Ray still got us there.
The nearby spring doesn't give it away,
Popping out like it does from solid
Rock, where even willows will not grow,
And diving underground before you know it,
As if it didn't like it here above.
What it looks like, in case we come up empty,
It looks small, just part of the woods, but small,
The cabin I mean, its logs obscured by brush.
It's dwarfed by the size of trunks surrounding it.
Deep snow country grows big trees. They vault
And loom in shadowed unconcern. The cabin
Is squalid, yes, but mostly it looks dim,
Or maybe brief would be the way to say it —
Depressing brevity we recognize
As squalor. Not much sun in woods like those,
None inside the windowless log shack.
Let's touch our horses up across this park.
That grove yonder might just be the one.
That time I came up here with Ray, God rest,
The time we found the place — it's only six
Or seven logs in height and ten-feet square —
The door was ajar and stingy with its dark.
I noticed that before I saw the roof
Caved in, which made that depth of dark seem strange.
It kind of chilled me when we found the spine
Of something human-sized right by the door.
Ray mentioned, *There's no need to close the door
Behind you if you're going out to die.*
It was half-buried. I'm not saying it

36

Was a man, just that it could have been.
I wouldn't know a spine of bear from man
Or woman, would you? I'll be damned. We're here.
It all looks just the same. The spine is gone.
What's that? A skull, sure as hell, half-buried,
Of half-unburied, like a blind white eye
In the ground. Relax. It isn't human.
More like an old badger. See the teeth? Here
The only human bones are yours and mine.

The Golden Room

WILFRID WILSON GIBSON

Do you remember that still summer evening
When, in the cosy cream-washed living-room
Of The Old Nailshop, we all talked and laughed —
Our neighbours from The Gallows, Catherine
And Lascelles Abercrombie; Rupert Brooke;
Eleanor and Robert Frost, living a while
At Little Iddens, who'd brought over with them
Helen and Edward Thomas? In the lamplight
We talked and laughed; but, for the most part, listened
While Robert Frost kept on and on and on,
In his slow New England fashion, for our delight,
Holding us with shrewd turns and racy quips,
And the rare twinkle of his grave blue eyes?

We sat there in the lamplight, while the day
Died from rose-latticed casements, and the plovers
Called over the low meadows, till the owls
Answered them from the elms, we sat and talked:
Now, a quick flash from Abercrombie; now,
A murmured dry half-heard aside from Thomas;
Now, a clear laughing word from Brooke; and then
Again Frost's rich and ripe philosophy,
That had the body and tang of good draught-cider,
And poured as dear a stream.
                                        'Twas in July
Of nineteen-fourteen that we sat and talked;
Then August brought the war, and scattered us.

Now, on the crest of an Ægean isle,
Brooke sleeps, and dreams of England: Thomas lies
'Neath Vimy Ridge, where he, among his fellows,
Died, just as life had touched his lips to song.

And nigh as ruthlessly has life divided
Us who survive; for Abercrombie toils
In a black Northern town, beneath the glower
Of hanging smoke; and in America
Frost farms once more; and, far from The Old Nailshop,
We sojourn by the Western sea.
                              And yet,
Was it for nothing that the little room,
All golden in the lamplight, thrilled with golden
Laughter from the hearts of friends that summer night?
Darkness has fallen on it; and the shadow
May never more be lifted from the hearts
That went through those black years of war, and live.

And still, whenever men and women gather
For talk and laughter on a summer night,
Shall not that lamp rekindle; and the room
Glow once again alive with light and laughter;
And, like a singing star in time's abyss,
Burn golden-hearted through oblivion?

Poetry's Beginning

GAIL HOSKING GILBERG

They visited Robert Frost's grave and came back
different people — she taller and he rounder.
The smooth stone with its list of Frost's children
and then the moon rising just short of the distant hills
invited them like a velvet couch. She wanted
to lie back on it so that Frost might whisper some truths
he knew but forgot to mention before this moment,
show them how *way leads on to way*
The fragrance of summer drifted all around.

For years afterwards they wondered why
the night ended at all, what it was
that made them return to town. They searched
for a coffee shop with lots of lights and
conversations that might lead them home again.
But the night was already old
and poetry was just beginning.

Quarreling with Robert Frost

MICHAEL S. GLASER

"Home is the place where, when you have to go there,
They have to take you in."
                    "I should have called it
Something you somehow haven't to deserve."
— Robert Frost, "The Death of the Hired Man"

I

What *I'd* call home
is that place where it was
safe enough to dream,
where we'd believe our parents
when they lied about the dark,

that place before our hearts
knew to doubt or question why,
and believed with passion

that nothing truly loved
would ever die.

II

Or were you talking of something else,
Robert Frost? For me, home is not
the place where they have to take you in,

so much as where,
when you have to go there
you can pretend

there is a there
to go to —
and often do.

Robert Frost's Writing Desk

DAVID GRAHAM

The Frost Place, Franconia, NH
For Don Sheehan

This rude contraption, two plain boards
nailed into a rough V then laid across
the arms of his Morris chair, makes all the rest
peripheral: windows bubbled with age,
sills littered with hundred year old flies,
wallpaper musty enough to be original,
the famous view rearing like an accusation.

Near the glass case with its book or two
signed by the great vanished hand,
I can sit where he sat, bowing to Lafayette
and its silent immensities, watching the moon
sail from treeless peak to hairy cloud.
I can murmur a verse or two
lived with so long they blot in advance
any of mine. He's many times gone,
and that may be why I dare fling myself
mothlike against his long guttered flame.
In this once unimaginable dusk,
Ridge Road dust figures forth, dimly real.

Poacher, squatter, phrase-thief — still
I do honor something here, even scratching
crooked words across the grain.
I honor no simple ghost, and look past
the slicing jealousies, the canny
maneuvering, platform tales told and told
so often they drifted moonlike
away from their own good light.

Despite July heat, I come to these sloping
floorboards, these shipwrecked shelves,
in search of first frost edging the wavering
glass or the muffled comfort of snowy
footprints across the yard
that wind has been dutifully erasing,
and air finally clear inside as out.

For the late R. F.

THOM GUNN

Without a net, eh? Orpheus then is
Mere player in a game of tennis?

Africa

MICHAEL HEFFERNAN

The only certain freedom's in departure.
— Robert Frost

I looked out toward the pasture at the cows
making their way from unknown hinterlands
to find themselves a shade-patch under trees
and look out toward the places they came from.
The shade was cool, the way shade often is
even in Africa, where I was not,
though Africa was often what I thought,
when I drove past the pasture into town
beyond the river next to the flood plain
where silent natives let their cattle move
among the egrets, geese, herons, and flies.
If this were Africa, what would I do
to live there? Would I simply roam about
from one place to another seeking shade
and company among the animals?
Should anyone attempt to live alone
in such a place as that? Would any place
be good enough to, without having to
pick up and wander continents from home?
What did I need to tell an animal?
What animal would want to talk to me?
What reasonable person thinks like this?
Once when my thoughts were roaring in my head
posing such questions for a mile or two
before I got to the next house up the road,
where someone like me stood by a chain-link fence
and a row of pines an ancient neighbor planted
to keep folks out, I knew I had no reason

to watch those cows again. The man I saw
had something in his hand, a knife or gun.
I thought I watched him turning in the mirror
twirling a sword above his head and screaming.
Beyond the pines, the warrior disappeared
into the world he came from. A cross of light
shook among boughs of gloom. I had to move,
at least to put new things in front of me,
if not to make another kind of home,
if home was what I wanted in the first place.
I'd call it by its name if it had one,
or, failing that, I'd call it Africa.

Frost Song

WILLIAM HEYEN

You weren't going to go insane, you said,
after your son's suicide — no matter what,
you'd endure. Now that you're dead,
we find the true center of your art

akin to stones you pried from ground
that often conspired (even for one versed
in country things) to fuse your exiled
heart into intonement, into sound.

Re: Robert

LARKIN HIGGINS

this night   unacquainted
delving intentions
figure   first lines   designer road
cored apples and birches' peeled skin
white
this page   preceding
accent of sense

the figure a poem makes   may be
another body

Unlettered

EDWARD J. INGEBRETSEN

Robert Frost's farm, Franconia, New Hampshire

When Robert Frost passed this stand of birch
Each gray curl held his eye at word-point.
No rock but gave him pause. He'd reach to touch
it where it lay. Stones taught him to roam
by showing him where he'd been. Freedom
to go meant knowing when and where to stay.

He leaned on the staff that time had carved clean.
It tensed beneath his weight; he leaned away
and his eye flicked like slow fire along the ridge.
A book there, said Frost, were you fierce enough
to read it. Life tells us plain what we need
to know. We live bounded or die being free.

See that field of corn across the road?
What truth it knows it does; it dies upward.
Or this spider, sifting like white smoke along
a stick of oak. Watch it. One point, then two —
any found place will do to make a home
if where you find yourself is someplace far.

Robert Frost wrote himself out of silence
and then back in. Words drew the point in lines.
Rocking on the porch (he was old even then),
he looked at the ridge a rock fall had cut.
See? he said. Write your scars like that.
Life's art is knowing what tells, not why.

Sprites

RICHARD JACKSON

Returning to the Frost Cabin, Ripton, Vermont

The night will be all dried moths on the windows.
The deer paths will wander off into furrows of darkness.
The moon will shipwreck the usual number of stars.
Which means how difficult it is to love you, because how easy.
When we look for our faces in the stream, they float away,
But even the most distant galaxies continue to tug on us.
Maybe time is the lumbering bear who forgets about
These winters, forgets about this dusk of blackbirds.
Maybe the thing I said tomorrow is preparing itself
Like that storm beyond the hills whose red sprites,
As they call them, which we can barely make out,
Those little flashes of electricity returning from the air
Back to earth, what Frost said was the right place
For love, returning what the sky had only borrowed,
Maybe they soak the grass like the sounds of crickets,
Maybe they are the words the hawk says to the mole.
Maybe all sprites remind us how easily our words evaporate.
I thought the rudder of the wind had broken loose.
I thought the moon had begun to unravel in your hands.
Or maybe this is just the way the evening dreams
About the morning. Maybe this is why we can barely
Speak our deepest hurts, but chatter like cracking branches
At what doesn't matter. Maybe our own dreams are
Just pine needles drifting down. We use them as kindling.
Tomorrow the light begins to spy on what this night has done.
Tomorrow we might say how our love, painted with these
Mismatched words, held back the darkness. There,
We've said it. So now maybe the wind will name each leaf,
The voices of birds will scatter their seeds, the stars will become

Sentences for our desires. It is at times like this I can
Walk into you as through the earth's door, to sleep
In its red clay, to lie drenched in the limbs of its words.

From the Porch of the Frost Place

GRAY JACOBIK

It is milkweed smells so sweet Peter and Joan tell me,
     and the last daylily's bloomed
in the bed that rims the porch. A single shrunken
     bloom, yesterday's, clings to a bare
forked stem among a forest of stems already withering.
     I notice melancholy's begun to veil
my thought because I can no longer shake a sight
     I caused last night returning
along Ridge Road — slammed my brakes but hit
     a chipmunk, not straight on,
but partially, and felt compelled to watch its grisly
     dance of flops until it stilled.
These small deaths, and the news of human ones
     constantly barraging us. And
now rumors of a second, coming war with Iraq.
     As always, the antinomies line up:
good, evil, but whose side is which? Last night Jessica
     read a poem about her friend,
in flames, choosing to throw herself from off one
     of the towers. Throughout the festival,
the trauma of last September's attack kept asserting
     itself, signaling how deeply scarred
we are. Lincoln's charge is on my mind, *to bind up*
     the nation's wounds, then Don
reminds us that yesterday was the anniversary
     of Hiroshima: that vast incineration —
was it 135,000 died in one great radiating ball
     of conflagration? We've heard
the justifying arguments all our lives, but they
     haven't redeemed an instant

of human suffering. The interest compounds *ad infinitum*:
    no moral nation can pay the debt.
Add it to our slavery debt, our genocide of native peoples
    debt, our bilking of The Third World debt.
Now a glider from Franconia's gliderport comes into view,
    circles around and across Lafayette
with its spill of rocks that each spring keeps a cross
    of not-yet melted snow.
Time to plant corn the locals say when the cross shows
    above the fields. How I wish
the Christian Cross had enough potency, after all these
    years, to have leached war-mongering
out of us. When our President signs the order to attack,
    he'll do it with God's blessing,
so he believes. I'd rather stake my faith in this creation
    before me, trusting that if there's
redemption and ease from suffering and grief, it comes
    in beholding this great blue dome
of sky, the varied mottling shadows and shapes of clouds,
    these blue-green mountains
and deep green hills, the pines and tamaracks, poplars,
    birches, the chipmunk who,
moment's ago, dared the porch, spotted me, scampered
    off in a scurry of cheeps. I want
to think he showed himself to forgive me for the maiming
    death of his kin, but that's
a fanciful wish that tells me I long for forgiveness this
    bright, clear, scintillate morning,
and I do, shameful, sorry creature that I am, who knows —
    but does not always abide by what
she knows — only one song is worthy of us and it is praise.

Robert Frost Discovers Another Road Not Taken

X. J. KENNEDY

Two roads diverged in a wood
As though in argument.
I had to keep going on one
To get to the end of a scent
That a nostril had begun,
But I picked out the no good.

What did it lead me to?
The old moose chewing her teat.
Still I'm bound to put up with Fate
Despite that aftermath.
I'd hold out for some kind of path
Under a body's feet.

Robert Frost

DAVID KEPLINGER

I rediscovered Frost at thirty-three.
He talked to me just like my father did.
I had the sense of Frost well memorized
By thirty-three. Another year and all
The meanings changed. Dear father at that age,
Made holy by a bulb in our garage,
You mend the arrows I have broken. You glue
The broken parts; you fix them in your hands
Like this, two fists. With twine you wrap each
Fracture so the glue will hold. I used to say:
I take them to the trash to hide my shame.
Enough. The glue holds well. The meanings give.
The sturdy arrows fly where I command.

For Robert Frost

GALWAY KINNELL

1

Why do you talk so much
Robert Frost? One day
I drove up to Ripton to ask,

I stayed the whole day
And never got the chance
To put the question.

I drove off at dusk
Worn out and aching
In both ears. Robert Frost,

Were you shy as a boy?
Do you go on making up
For some long period of solitude?

Is it that talk
Doesn't have to be metered and rhymed?
Or is talk distracting from something worse?

2

I saw you once on the TV,
Unsteady at the lectern,
The flimsy white leaf
Of hair standing straight up
In the wind, among top hats,
Old farmer and son
Of worse winters than this,
Stopped in the first dazzle

Of the District of Columbia,
Suddenly having to pay
For the cheap onionskin,
The worn-out ribbon, the eyes
Wrecked from writing poems
For us — stopped,
Lonely before millions,
The paper jumping in your grip,

And as the Presidents
Also on the platform
Began flashing nervously
Their Presidential smiles
For the harmless old guy,
And poets watching on the TV
Started thinking, Well that's
The end of *that* tradition,

And the managers of the event
Said, Boys this is it,
This sonofabitch poet
Is gonna croak,
Putting the paper aside
You drew forth
From your great faithful heart
The poem.

3

Once, walking in winter in Vermont,
In the snow, I followed a set of footprints
That aimed for the woods. At the verge
I could make out, "far in the pillared dark,"
An old creature in a huge, clumsy overcoat,
Lifting his great boots through the drifts,
Going as if to die among "those dark trees"
Of his own country. I watched him go,

Past a house, quiet, warm and light,
A farm, a countryside, a woodpile in its slow
Smokeless burning, alder swamps ghastly white,
Tumultuous snows, blanker whitenesses,
Into the pathless wood, one eye weeping,
The dark trees, for which no saying is dark enough,
Which mask the gloom and lead on into it,
The bare, the withered, the deserted.

There were no more cottages.
Soft bombs of dust falling from the boughs,
The sun shining no warmer than the moon,
He had outwalked the farthest city light,
And there, clinging to the perfect trees,
A last leaf. What was it?
What was that whiteness? — white, uncertain —
The night too dark to know.

4

He turned. *Love,*
Love of things, duty, he said,
And made his way back to the shelter
No longer sheltering him, the house
Where everything turned to words,

Where he would think on the white wave,
Folded back, that rides in place on the obscure
Pouring of this life to the sea —
And seal the broken lips
Of darkness with the *mot juste.*

5

Poet of the country of white houses,
Of clearings going out to the dark wall of woods
Frayed along the skyline, you who nearly foreknew

The next lines of poems you suddenly left off writing,
Who dwelt in access to that which other men
Have burned all their lives to get near, who heard
The high wind, in gusts, seething
From far off, coming through the trees exactly
To this place where it must happen, who spent
Your life on the point of giving yourself away
To the dark trees, the dissolving woods,
Into which you go at last, heart in hand, deep in:
When we think of a man who was cursed
Neither with the all-lovingness of Walt Whitman
Nor with Melville's anguish to know and to suffer,
And yet cursed . . . A man, what shall I say,
Vain, not fully convinced he was dying, whose calling
Was to set up in the wilderness of his country,
At whatever cost, a man who would be his own man,
We think of you. And from the same doorway
At which you lived, between the house and the woods,
We see your old footprints going away across
The great Republic, Frost, up memorized slopes,
Down hills floating by heart on the bulldozed land.

Mending Sump

KENNETH KOCH

"Hiram, I think the sump is backing up.
The bathroom floor boards for above two weeks
Have seemed soaked through. A little bird, I think
Has wandered in the pipes, and all's gone wrong."
"Something there is that doesn't hump a sump,"
He said; and through his head she saw a cloud
That seemed to twinkle. "Hiram, well," she said,
"Smith is come home! I saw his face just now
While looking through your head. He's come to die
Or else to laugh, for hay is dried-up grass
When you're alone." He rose, and sniffed the air,
"We'd better leave him in the sump," he said.

Bending the Light

TOM KOONTZ

some boy's been swinging them

the ground is shadowy moist
below him, the world blazing
in the fields far out through space
between summering leaves. And

yes he's been haunted by the good
ghost of *climbing*, like climbing
the world, *mostly too high*
in the oaks to swing out but
sometimes *in the small elms*,
the small arms of a day, *his body*
carries back, hands loving

the rough bark of shovels and
hammers, jokes, boots, books,
cheers, khakis, *launching outward*
with lectures and hymns, ties, vows,
baptisms, giggles, sobs, t-shirts, *and*
downward through warnings, wills,
counsels, prescriptions, robes, phone
calls and letters, *looking to ground*
on dependable earth. But no, at 75

still he's climbing, *climbing*, trying
to bend some light across a line
of the straighter, darker thing.

Dark and Deep

NORBERT KRAPF

When Robert Frost walked
in the woods he had a sense
of where the trail would fork
but not where the branches
would lead or what darkness
or light or shading of the two
might lie beyond and it was
the thrill of not knowing where
he was going or what might come
that gave a slight bounce to his step
as the dusk thickened and the dark
began to pull him on like a magnet
at the back of a deep cave where
shadows flickered like a campfire
and he loved to stand in a hollow
as if at the bottom of a well
and look up at the snowflakes
falling heavily out of a starless
sky landing on his eyelashes
and part of him wanted to stay
there forever and just gaze
as the woods filled with snow
and part of him said you better
leave soon and the only way
he could find his way back
to where he had started from
was to compose in his mind
in a language he had to discover
a poem whose lines snaked
out of the dark and whose

rhythms moved his feet
to take the steps that led back
to where others liked to walk
and promises could be kept.

The Final Poem

MAXINE KUMIN

Bread Loaf, late August, the chemistry
of a New England fall already
inviting the swamp maples to flare.

Magisterial in the white wicker rocker
Robert Frost at rest after giving
a savage reading

holding nothing back, his rage
at dying, *not yet,* as he barged
his chair forth, then back, *don't sit*

there mumbling in the shadows, call
yourselves poets? All
but a handful scattered. Fate

rearranged us happy few at his feet.
He rocked us until midnight. I took
away these close-lipped dicta. *Look*

up from the page. Pause between poems.
Say something about the next one.
Otherwise the audience

will coast, they can 't take in
half of what you're giving them.
Reaching for the knob of his cane

he rose and flung this exit line:
Make every poem your final poem.

A Hundred Himalayas

SYDNEY LEA

And miles to go

I stop for breath at height of land — not much
at that, a loaflike clump, the likes of which

I'd have sneered at, younger. Forgive the body's failures,
I think, you've climbed a hundred Himalayas,

hill by hill in 60 years. My dog
must think it queer, that I should stop so long....

No, that's the sentimentalist, allusion-
monger. No thought in a dog, hence no confusion.

He does what he does, or rather, what I do.
Beast's obedience. And what have I to show

that's so much different? Which is not to say
I have peculiar reason to complain.

I don't. I'm standing here. Meanwhile one of my brothers
lies long since buried, and in this single winter

the Crab has clawed too many else to count.
"From the rising up of the sun to the going down,"

I've read, "The mighty God has called the world."
Indeed. Not mighty myself, I choose to hail

the things that are, like time, and death, and love.
Above all love. In a nearby stump, a groove

holds something shining: a perfect jewel of quartz —
purple, enduring, shaped somewhat like a heart.

The day's sufficient to the day. A simple stone....
I conquer my small Everests one by one.

January 20

DAVID LEHMAN

When Robert Frost recited "The Gift Outright"
in the gleaming cold noonday sun I was watching
there was no school I don't remember why
that afternoon we played touch football, my friends and I
on a sloping meadow in Fort Tryon Park
and life was going on elsewhere, life was going on downtown
in night clubs that even then were going out of fashion
like the Stork Club or El Morocco and my friends and I
wanted to grow up and smoke cigarettes and drink highballs
and buy fur coats for our wives and take them to clubs
because that was life, and what we didn't realize
was that our afternoon in Fort Tryon Park
where we got into a fight with some Irish kids
was also life and even then was turning
into history with the Bay of Pigs and the Vienna summit
and Berlin and the missile crisis and the speech in Berlin
and the discotheques that put the night clubs out of business
and Sam Giancana, the mob boss who would have
ordered a hit on Sinatra except he wanted
to hear him sing "Chicago" one more time

The Night Robert Frost Died

LYN LIFSHIN

I was riding around Albany
in an always breaking down
sports car, as if I could get
away from those Vermont
doom filled hills, the green
pastures of Frost's coming back
so many years later in my new
book of horse poems, his leaves,
leaves in the first poem I wrote.
I thought as the dry leaves
blew thru our red car how
Frost made himself a part,
hiding behind a face of tearing
words, mourning the agitated
heart. I tried to escape that.
I've got a good mask too.
That night I was probably
laughing, looking for a new
place to try to make home.
Part of me never leaves
Middlebury, Robert in his
baggy green pants carrying
strawberries, letting only my
father wait on him in Lazarus
Dept Store. Two cold quiet
men who could sit years
alone in a house of people
never saying a word. Sliding
thru Albany, looking for a
place for a beer, the Boulevard
I was thinking of a first poem

I wrote in 3rd grade, the one
my father gave to Frost
who wrote on it, "very good images"
and then "bring me some more,"
and how my poems have filled with
apple boughs, blossoms,
apple trees, how I've lived on
Appletree Lane, Rapple Drive,
had apples on my glasses
and of course apples in
the horse poems. "No joy but
lacks salt that is not dusted
with pain," Frost said and I see
that staining my poems. Was
it his "Cow in Apple Time," the
cider syrup, the sweet fruit after blossoms
or the fruit rotting, the darkness, the ache, the
ice the snow and the snow in each kiss
or lip or finger that hooked me?

My Test Market

RACHEL LODEN

I sha'n't be gone long. — You come too.
— Robert Frost

Let's fly off to Finland, far
from the long arm of Olestra. There

in bog, arctic fen, and sand
are others who may understand

our epic innocence. Oh, how many
names for snow! and none

with growing market share. Where
are the snows that make no sense

so early in the morning, when the snow
is blue and blowing on the steppes?

Where is the *qanisqineg*,
the 'snow floating on water'?

We may ask Vigdís Finnbogadóttir,
who's not a Finn. She may not know,

but she may point us toward
the northern lights. Her aim is true,

her snowshoes always full of snow.
We won't come back. You come too.

Robert Frost

ROBERT LOWELL

Robert Frost at midnight, the audience gone
to vapor, the great act laid on the shelf in mothballs,
his voice is musical and raw — he writes in the flyleaf:
For Robert from Robert, his friend in the art.
"Sometimes I feel too full of myself," I say.
And he, misunderstanding, "When I am low,
l stray away. My son wasn't your kind. The night
we told him Merrill Moore would come to treat him,
he said, 'I'll kill him first.' One of my daughters thought things,
thought every male she met was out to make her;
the way she dressed, she couldn't make a whorehouse."
And I, "Sometimes I'm so happy I can't stand myself."
And he, "When I am too full of joy, I think
how little good my health did anyone near me."

"Found Poem," North of Boston

PAUL MARION

FROST
HEAVES

Winter, 1963

DAVID MASON

As my father turned the car into the drive
and we were home from our rare trip to church,
a man's voice speaking from the radio
caused us to linger there, engine running.
Just so, the voice with its calm cadences
lingered by woods where snow fell downily.

Though only eight, I thought I understood
the words to fit our snowless January,
and that the man, whose name was Robert Frost
(like rime I saw that morning on the lawn),
had died in Boston, which was far away.

Who knows where I went next, with all the woods
about the house to play in, but I recall
the chilling dullness of the winter sky
and firs so still I almost heard them breathing.
I thought it wasn't Jack, but Robert, Frost,
who made them live in such a cold repose.

Within two weeks another poet died,
her head in a cold gas oven. No poem
of hers was broadcast to my family.
Years would pass before I learned her name.

The old man in his woods, the young mother
dying with two children near — such vanity
and madness framed the choices both had made —
the way he stuck it out, the way she lost it.

I've tried to cast my lot with that old man,
but something in her fate tugs at me too.
She can't have known the *cause célèbre* she'd be,
wanting to leave the world for leaving her.

The world goes on despite us and our poems,
snow falling in woods, or not falling,
lights coming on in houses, lights going out,
but I feel grateful that my father stopped
the car that January day, his head
almost bowed as he left the radio on.

On the Porch at the Frost Place, Franconia, NH

WILLIAM MATTHEWS

For Stanley Plumly

So here the great man stood,
fermenting malice and poems
we have to be nearly as fierce
against ourselves as he
not to misread by their disguises.
Blue in dawn haze, the tamarack
across the road is new since Frost
and thirty feet tall already.
No doubt he liked to scorch off
morning fog by simply staring through it
long enough so that what he saw
grew visible. "Watching the dragon
come out of the Notch," his children
used to call it. And no wonder
he chose a climate whose winter
and house whose isolation could be
stern enough to his wrath and pity
as to make them seem survival skills
he'd learned on the job, farming
fifty acres of pasture and woods.
For cash crops he had sweat and doubt
and moralizing rage, those staples
of the barter system. And these swift
and aching summers, like the blackberries
I've been poaching down the road
from the house where no one's home —
acid at first and each little globe
of the berry too taut and distinct
from the others, then they swell to hold

the riot of their juices and briefly
the fat berries are perfected to my taste,
and then they begin to leak and blob
and under their crescendo of sugar
I can taste how they make it through winter....
By the time I'm back from a last,
six-berry raid, it's almost dusk,
and more and more mosquitoes
will race around my ear their tiny engines,
the speedboats of the insect world.
I won't be longer on the porch
than it takes to look out once
and see what I've taught myself
in two months here to discern:
night restoring its opacities,
though for an instant as intense
and evanescent as waking from a dream
of eating blackberries and almost
being able to remember it, I think
I see the parts — haze, dusk, light
broken into grains, fatigue,
the mineral dark of the White Mountains,
the wavering shadows steadying themselves —
separate, then joined, then seamless:
the way, in fact, Frost's great poems,
like all great poems, conceal
what they merely know, to be
predicaments. However long
it took to watch what I thought
I saw, it was dark when I was done,
everywhere and on the porch,
and since nothing stopped
my sight, I let it go.

Robert Frost as Father

SARAH KATHERINE MCCANN

Getting your kids to climb
ropes — the barn so splintered
wood under the wool —
and through the dark they find
what you tossed up on the hay —
you're an old white father against
the black sky tipping stories
from your chair — stacking your stone
walls hand over hand
horses all around — letting the farm
farm itself — your children twisting
into the fields — the fields
twisting into their hair farther
and whenever they stole peaches
from the trees you made
them plant the pits.

Robert Frost in Warsaw

PETER MEINKE

When I saw birches in Wasienki Park
leaning against the wind, I thought of you,
old ghost, so strongly have you claimed those trees
for us. Even here, four thousand miles away
from Derry or Franconia, your voice,
through foreign though familiar leaves, whispers
that the human heart can neither forfeit
nor accept responsibilities. Even
here, where storms far wilder, blacker, than those
which strike New Hampshire have torn up the stones
and thrown uncounted populations
into hells we only read about, your poems
proclaim ambiguous affirmation
in the dark. I sit here in a rented room
with you, heart pumping as I read your lines,
and think of parents, wife, and children
who travel with me complicated roads
beneath a winter sky that hides the stars.
They tell me you were selfish: it may be so.
I know you spoke to me through birches in
Wasienki Park, kindly, and brought me home.

In Memory of Robert Frost

WILLIAM MEREDITH

Everyone had to know something, and what they said
About that, the thing they'd learned by curious heart,
They said well.
           That was what he wanted to hear,
Something you had done too exactly for words,
Maybe, but too exactly to lie about either.
Compared to such talk, most conversation
Is inadvertent, low-keyed lying.

If he walked in fear of anything, later on
(Except death, which he died with a healthy fear of)
It was that he would misspeak himself. Even his smile
He administered with some care, accurately.
You could not put words in his mouth
And when you quoted him in his presence
There was no chance that he would not contradict you.

Then there were apparent samenesses he would not
Be deceived by. The presidents of things,
Or teachers, braggarts, poets
Might offer themselves in stereotype
But he would insist on paying attention
Until you at least told him an interesting lie.
(That was perhaps your field of special knowledge?)
The only reason to lie, he said, was for a purpose:
To get something you wanted that bad.

I told him a couple — to amuse him,
To get something I wanted, his attention?
More likely, respite from that blinding attention,
More likely, a friendship
I felt I could only get by stealing.

What little I'd learned about flying
Must have sweated my language lean. *I'd respect you*
For that if for nothing else, he said not smiling
The time I told him, thirty-two night landings
On a carrier, or thirty-two night catapult shots —
Whatever it was, true, something I knew.

Robert Frost's Chair

GARY METRAS

Derry, New Hampshire
For Wally Swist

He would rest his elbows
and the writing desk he made
on the flat maple wood arms.
He sank into the gold and green
flowery cushions, like sitting
in a meadow in August
as goldenrod bloom.
From the impression he left
in the seat, you can tell
he chose the way less
traveled and journeyed
miles and miles in that chair.
The hay unmowed,
the wall unmended,
cows to milk at midnight,
but the notebooks fat,
leaking words all
over the carpet.

Interpretation of a Poem by Frost

THYLIAS MOSS

A young black girl stopped by the woods,
so young she knew only one man: Jim Crow
but she wasn't allowed to call him Mister.
The woods were his and she respected his boundaries
even in the absence of fence.
Of course she delighted in the filling up
of his woods, she so accustomed to emptiness,
to being taken at face value.
This face, her face eternally the brown
of declining autumn, watches snow inter the grass,
cling to bark making it seem indecisive
about race preference, a fast-to-melt idealism.
With the grass covered, black and white are the only options,
polarity is the only reality; corners aren't neutral
but are on edge.
She shakes off snow, defiance wasted
on the limited audience of horse.
The snow does not hypnotize her as it wants to,
as the blond sun does in making too many prefer daylight.
She has promises to keep,
the promise that she bear Jim no bastards,
the promise that she ride the horse only as long
as it is willing to accept riders,
the promise that she bear Jim no bastards,
the promise to her face that it not be mistaken as shadow,
and miles to go, more than the distance from Africa to Andover
more than the distance from black to white
before she sleeps with Jim.

For Robert Frost, in the Autumn, in Vermont

HOWARD NEMEROV

All on the mountains, as on tapestries
Reversed, their threads unreadable though clear,
The leaves turn in the volume of the year.
Your land becomes more brilliant as it dies.

The puzzled pilgrims come, car after car,
With cameras loaded for epiphanies;
For views of failure to take home and prize,
The dying tourists ride through realms of fire.

"To die is gain," a virgin's tombstone said;
That was New England, too, another age
That put a higher price on maidenhead
if brought in dead; now on your turning page
The lines blaze with a constant light, displayed
As in the maple's cold and fiery shade.

Frost's Last Lecture: A Tape: His Audience — 1963

WILLIAM OLSEN

They are listening to what he hears. They are long ago.
They step into the lecture, it's never the same twice.

The cough, the rustle of a chair, the common laughter
breaking up, intake, labored pause, the obstinate sigh ...

they are listening to what they heard and what he heard.
He seems too lost in his notes to go the rest of the way.

Let them go to the wolves, he said of those who can't keep up.
You could almost hear those wolves, their shattered breath.

The gist seems always so, clear, if anything is clear.
One sentence at a time, he keeps saying goodbye. . . .

Don't sympathize with it too much an old voice said.
Extravagance is meager acts and subtler inactions,

pursuit or escape, of the broken world, broken love.
Ordained or not, they've failed, it must be made better.

But first they must freely submit to their essence and
all over again ENDURE their freedom: extravagance:

sometimes it's remorse, sometimes it's nearly hope,
sometimes it's something they couldn't bear to hope.

"Fire and Ice" by Robert Frost: an early draft

RON OVERTON

Some say the world will end in fire,

Some say in ice.

But from my experience of (muck and mire,) / taste?   sense?

I give the nod to lusty fire,   /cocksure?

Flamboyant as dyslectic mice.   / these dancing mice? χ

But on the other hand I'd hate

To slight the might of mighty ice.

Its heavy weight   work *muskrat ramble* into poem?

Would also suffice.

~~end things nice?~~

Look up! Doubleplay combination? ? ? (sounds familiar!)

(perhaps mice should be left out altogether?)

I love this line!

84

The Ruined House

JAY PARINI

Deep in the woods, beyond the shuffle
of our works and days, we found a path
between an alley of Norwegian pines.
The children ran on spongy needles,
disappearing in the purple shade;
their shouts were lost among the bird-yip:
tremolo of wood-doves, long diphthong
of redwing blackbirds, crass old crows
all harping on the same old note again.
Your hand in mine, we seemed to drift upon
a fuzzy cumulous of half-voiced thoughts:
the tongue's quick shuttle through the loom of mind
in search of texture, text to sing,
recitativo of a thousand glimpses
caught, composed. All along the way
the eye sought gleanings, images to tell,
to cast one's thoughts on, fix the swell
of meaning in the cross-haired sights
of metaphor, a trope to end all troping:
words and things in pure performance.

Now the hilly path went straightaway ahead,
unfolding with the ease of morning vision.
As they would, the children found it first:
the ruined house on what was once
a breezy hillock in an open field.
The coarse foundation might have been
a dry stone wall like other walls
now winding over hills, down dingly dells,
to parse the complex sentence of our past,
delineating fields no longer found,

obscured by popple, tamarack and vetch.
The stone foundation of the house in ruins
wasn't stern or morally suggestive.
It had just withstood what it could stand —
the falling stars, the tumbledown of snow,
sharp dislocations of the frosty ground,
the weight of timber soaking in the rain.

We stepped inside behind the children,
who were walking beams like tightrope wires
across a corridor that once led somewhere
warm, familial, and full of light.
The cellarhole was still a hutch of night:
one saw it through the intermittent floorboards
and the two-by-fours exposed like vertebrae
that once held everything in place
but powdered now and sagged toward the middle
as the woodmites fed and moisture softened
grainy fibers, as the mulch of days
began in earnest. There was still a roof
aloft amid the trees, a fragile shade
with patches that were open into sky.
The children clambered up a tilting stairwell
to the second floor; we followed suit,
though not so fearessly and free
of old conceptions — hurtful images
that hold one back, making one wish
for something less or something more.

The little bedrooms that we found upstairs
were still intact, with built-in beds,
coarse empty shelves still half considering
the weight of objects from their rumored past.
If one stood still and listened close
the voices of the children could be heard,
their laughter in the leaves, the sass and chatter.

Anyway, that's what I told the children,
who believed and listened and could hear.
It's not so hard to frame the past
upon the present, to connect the dots
all still in place, to resurrect and ride
ancestral voices: there is one great tongue.
We find ourselves alive in that old mouth,
through which all meaning flows to sea.
We pour and pour the water of our lives,
a glittery cascade, its brightness falling
into pools where it must darken once again,
must soak in soil, collect and gather
in a place to tap for future soundings.

Later, in the shade behind the house,
we lingered in the garden's dense enclosure.
Petalfall of spring was planted there,
the hard ground turned, the weeds uprooted.
Beans and flowers were assigned to rows.
While he would ditch the upper pasture,
she was left alone sometimes in summer
and would sit there safely in the chestnut shade
to read the Brownings, he and she,
as children napped or slaughtered dragons
with their makeshift swords. That's how the idyll
runs, of course. The typhus and the cold
that cracked the windowpanes in mid-November
and the bitter words: these, too, were true.

We left on hushing feet like thieves
with something in our pockets, awed and fragile.
It was only time that turned those pages,
leaving dust in sunlight on the stairs,
disfiguring the walls that once would keep
a family aloft through hazy fall
and hardy winter into sopping spring.

It was only time that would not stop,
that bore us homeward of the needle path
toward the end of what was ours
a while that summer in the leafy woods.

Remembering Frost at Kennedy's Inauguration

LINDA PASTAN

Even the flags seemed frozen
to their poles, and the men
stamping their well shod feet
resembled an army of overcoats.

But we were young and fueled
by hope, our ardor burned away
the cold. We were the president's,
and briefly the president would be ours.

The old poet stumbled
over his own indelible words,
his breath a wreath around his face:
a kind of prophecy.

Stray Moth, Asleep

JOYCE PESEROFF

Exotic thumbalina, crayola flame,
soft yellow grub with pink antennae,
rose and saffron wings shut like tent-flaps,
scrap of a girl's dress, secret as a tulip
or wildflower still buttoned at the neck,

on the doorframe all day you're naked
prey, still zonked at half past five — nothing
like Frost's white-on-white papery stiff.
Accident dropped from a cloud, your silk
parachute opens to no comrade or lover.

What night-blooming thing waits for you?
 — yet not for you, exactly; wherever
you were hijacked from, brothers bunch
like clover on a Lamb Festival float. No judge
notices one missing, or a hole in the design.

Thanks, Robert Frost

DAVID RAY

Do you have hope for the future ?
someone asked Robert Frost, toward the end.
Yes, and even for the past, he replied,
that it will turn out to have been all right
for what it was, something we can accept,
mistakes made by the selves we had to be,
not able to be, perhaps, what we wished,
or what looking back half the time it seems
we could so easily have been, or ought . . .
The future, yes, and even for the past,
that it will become something we can bear.
And I too, and my children, so I hope,
will recall as not too heavy the tug
of those albatrosses I sadly placed
upon their tender necks. *Hope for the past*,
yes, old Frost, your words provide that courage,
and it brings strange peace that itself passes
into past, easier to bear because
you said it, rather casually, as snow
went on falling in Vermont years ago.

The Illusion

F. D. REEVE

We came out to a clearing in the rain;
across the field the mountains lay in view,
lords of the world, self-confident like god.
In the valley we heard the whistle of a passing train.

The clouds slid quickly on, the sun burst like a shout,
the crenellated peaks pushed up the sky;
the earth in our hands, the breathless seeing
laid us like giants across the wet grass flat.

Slowly the weather closed, the fog rolled in,
the trees shut down behind gray skirts of rain;
the world in our palms disappeared in the heavy air,
and the mountains vanished like a soundless train.

The Blue Plate Tea Room: Sestina

JOHN RIDLAND

When Robert Frost came barding down to Hartford,
Some middle meddler rang up Wallace Stevens
To meet for lunch at some "place called The Blue Plate
Tea Room, because there was no other place,"
Wrote Stevens.* In October '42
You let things roll the way they had to roll.

They couldn't welcome Frost with fife and drum roll.
And as for what they'd eat in wartime Hartford, —
Butter was rationed, back in '42
(You wouldn't know it, though, to look at Stevens,
Or Frost) — I'd guess, at that time, in that place,
Both of them muttered, "Well. I'll take the Blue Plate

Special" (which must have been served *on* a blue plate,
One pitty-pat of margarine per roll).
The waitress slung them down each in their place.
"How do you do it, Wally, here in Hartford?"
Frost would have chaffed him, looking hard at Stevens,
And laughed a laugh pure 1942.

We still make movies set in '42.
Their soundtracks catch the clatter of The Blue Plate
But so far haven't dubbed the words of Stevens,
Which could have been, "*Ça va*. The barrel roll
Is not attempted often now in Hartford.
What do you say we drive past Clemens' place?"

Their conversation's one you can't quite place,
Stamped with the dateline 1942.
TWO POETS MEET AND EAT, the Daily Hartford
Times could have had it: "In the modest Blue Plate
Tea Room, two men securely on the roll
Of poets, Robert Frost and Wallace Stevens ..."

Later, as afternoon rolled under, Stevens
Wrote Frost he hoped that some time out at his place
(Asylum Avenue) they'd eat an eggroll
Of Blue Plate language, saved from '42,
And say goodbye just like they'd left The Blue Plate,
Shaking big hands in Anglo-Saxon Hartford.

Envoy: The Shooting Script

SCENE: Hartford. CU SHOT OF Wallace Stevens
Inside The Blue Plate Tea Room — dumpy place.
OUTSIDE: a '42 Ford. Frost steps down. *ROLL 'EM!*

Letters of Wallace Stevens, p. 423.

Elinor Frost's Marble-Topped Kneading Table

PATTIANN ROGERS

Imagine that motion, the turning and pressing,
the constant folding and overlapping, the dough
swallowing and swallowing and swallowing itself
again, just as the sea, bellying up the hard shore,
draws back under its own next forward-moving
roll, slides out from under itself
along the beach and back again; that first
motion, I mean, like the initial act
of any ovum (falcon, leopard, crab) turning
into itself, taking all of its outside surfaces
inward; the same circular mixing and churning
and straightening out again seen at the core
of thunderheads born above deserts; that involution
ritualized inside amaryllis bulbs
and castor beans in May.

Regard those hands now, if you never
noticed before, flour-caked fists and palms knuckling
the lump, gathering, dividing, tucking
and rolling, smoothing, reversing. I know,
from the stirring and sinking habits
of your own passions, that you recognize
this motion.

And far in the distance (you may even
have guessed), far past Orion and Magellan's vapors,
past the dark nebulae and the sifted rings
of interstellar dust, way beyond mass and propulsion,
before the first wheels and orbits of sleep
and awareness, there, inside that moment
which comes to be, when we remember,
at the only center where it has always been,

an aproned figure stands kneading, ripe
with yeast, her children at her skirts.
Now and then she pauses, bends quickly,
clangs open the door, tosses another stick
on the fire.

Robert Frost to Ezra Pound's Daughter from His Deathbed

GIBBONS RUARK

Love is all. I tremble with it.
Romantic love as in stones and poems.
I'd like to see Ezra again.

Did I say stones? My mind said stories
And my tremulous tongue said stones.
Love is all I tremble with. It

Goes without saying I am gone.
Before I go for good I'll say
I'd like to see Ezra. Again

The years, the years rattle my spine.
How often must I not know what
Love is? All I tremble with, it

Rummages these old bones, scattering
Breath like the silvered leaves of birches
I'd like to see. Ezra? Again

His crazed head haunts me like a cloud.
All the dark certainties tell me
Love is all. I tremble with it.
I'd like to see Ezra again.

Double Dialogue: Homage to Robert Frost

MURIEL RUKEYSER

In agony saying : "The last night of his life,
My son and I in the kitchen : At half-past one
He said, 'I have failed as a husband. Now my wife
Is ill again and suffering.' At two
He said, 'I have failed as a farmer, for the sun
Is never there, the rain is never there.'
At three he said, 'I have failed as a poet who
Has never not once found my listener.
There is no sense to my life.' But then he heard me out.
I argued point by point. Seemed to win. Won.
He spoke to me once more when I was done:
'Even in argument, father, I have lost.'
He went and shot himself. Now tell me this one thing:
Should I have let him win then? Was I wrong?"

To answer for the land for love for song
Arguing life for life even at your life's cost.

Robert Frost

LEX RUNCIMAN

But for pictures
and the memory-twisted reminiscences
of others, I never knew him.
I know when he died, 1963
the day after my father's birthday.
I was twelve and remember
reading the dying
newspaper tribute.
And I remember one day,
January, his standing
in the black box of our television,
holding a paper
gone suddenly white
and silent in cold sun.
So he put it down
and began reciting
"The Gift Outright"
into the clear air, a public man
talking the way I believed a private man
would talk, if he ever did.

Why God Chose Robert Frost over Elvis

LYNN VEACH SADLER

God made man in His image, true,
but after the Beginning,
He needed an image of Himself for men,
a "persona," as it were, and chose Robert Frost
(who looked much more dignified than he was).

But Elvis was Runner-Up
and all the Honorable Mentions.
The angels say, off the record,
it would have been beneath God's dignity
to commit to Elvisonian gyration,
which would have put to consternation
every solitary constellation.

Besides, Rob deliberately made himself
the ram caught in the thicket by his horns
when he ran around sprinkling "Grace Notes"
throughout New Hampshire.
And, to offset his rival's blue suede shoes,
he adopted *blue* Keds Casuals
(in canvas, with white rubber soles,
which he deliberately misspelled).

Elvis sang all those holy songs,
such as "Amazing Grace,"
and had Grace*land*, true,
but his handicap was (and is)
that he keeps coming back on his own.
If God were to come down as Elvis,
He wouldn't know if He's coming or going!

And there was that time when Elvis,
abetted by a "Jeroboam" of strong drink,
burst in on Mr. Nixon with Jeremiads
against drugs, Hippies, and the Beatles.

Elvis knew doubles (but God is into *triples*).
His twin brother, Jesse Garon Presley,
died at birth, but some say, and doubtless believe,
he took Elvis's place at the time Elvis joined the Army.
The real Elvis came back when Jesse-Garon-died-
when-people-think-Elvis-died.
The one humans keep sighting is the real Elvis
trying to make up for all those lost years.

Elvis was anointed "King" (if not "King of Kings")
through his appearances on the Louisiana Hayride.
From it, he toured the South, made it explode, and
left hill- and rockabilly deified.

But God is God and fair. For being Runner-Up
and all Honorable Mentions, Elvis was made
the Man in the Moon and still gets
to come back as himself, while,
the angels say, Rob had rather come back
as himself than God.

Frost at Midnight

MARY JO SALTER

> *For I was reared*
> *In the great city, pent 'mid cloisters dim,*
> *And saw nought lovely but the sky and stars.*
> *But thou, my babe! shalt wander like a breeze*
> *By lakes and sandy shores . . .*
> — Coleridge

1.

His children tuckered out, tucked in (three girls
jammed in one bedroom, the boy in the only other),
and Elinor dozing where the dining room
would be if they'd had room, the "Yank from Yankville,"
as he liked to call himself, was wide awake.
It was midnight, on the fifteenth of September,
1912, and Frost was thirty-eight.
Tonight, he'd stay up late before the fire
in his Morris chair, as he often did, and write
to Susan Hayes Ward of *The Independent*,
who'd been the first to put his name in print.
Hard to believe that he, New Hampshire teacher
and half-hearted farmer, poet of little note,
just days before had boarded *The Parisian*
from Boston to Glasgow, then taken the train to London
with all of those now sleeping in his care.
Or that a tip from a retired policeman
(they knew no one in England, not a soul)
had led them to the village of Beaconsfield,
and a cottage called The Bungalow (or Bung Hole,
in the family lingo) for a monthly rent
of twenty dollars. Why were they here?

They'd flipped a coin.
Heads England, tails Vancouver — the nickel rose
silver like the moon from the Atlantic
they'd cross, sea-sick, to see it land again.
And now they lived behind a looming hedge
of American laurel, taller than any he
had seen at home. He wasn't here to pose
at Englishness, although the place was quaint,
all right: the muffin man had stepped
out of the nursery rhyme to walk their street
with the flypaper man; the knife-grinder; the man
who dangled pots and pans for sale from a wagon
drawn by a donkey. All this the children loved,
and Elinor might still fulfill her dream
sometime of sleeping under thatch. But no,
he hadn't come to write about such things.
At the bottom of his trunk the manuscripts
of some hundred poems waited to be sorted
into two books or three, and he'd write more
about the world he knew and had left behind.

His firstborn Elliott dead (his fault, he thought —
he'd called for the wrong doctor); later a daughter,
her mother's namesake, who lived not quite two days —
he wouldn't stop to brood on those troubles now.
Tonight his mood was defiant, even "aberrant,"
he wrote to Susan Ward. He'd "achieve something
solid enough to sandbag editors with."
After all, it was just a few miles from here
that Milton, in a cottage like this (shared
with *his* three daughters) finished *Paradise Lost*.
And a mile or two the other way that Gray,
redeemed by glory, lay in a country churchyard.
"To London town what is it but a run?"
he closed in singsong, adding he'd step out

to the yard, before bed, to watch the city lights
in the distance "flaring like a dreary dawn."

Not quite — but a visionary flourish?
A biographer named Walsh, who went to live
in The Bungalow long after, noted how
London remains some twenty-one miles off.
Equipped with a naked eye, then, Frost could never
have caught the faintest glimmer of the city.
But was this the night the first biographer
would write of as the turning point? The night
the poems were taken from the trunk and sorted
into the first of all the selves he left?
It was sometime in September or October.
Frost sat on the cold floor. From time to time,
he'd crumple a ball and toss it in the fire.
He saw, in the hearth, the lights of London blaze
each time he found a poem to sacrifice:
that way the ones he saved could shine the brighter.
Or it may be, as the curling pages turned
brilliant a fierce instant, then to ash,
he was thinking of the sallow leaves that fell
indifferently outside, beyond the laurel,
and was terrified of their unwritten message.
By October's end, the book was done and out,
typed by his eldest, Lesley; a Mrs. Nutt
(who shrugged "the day of poetry is past")
allowed she was nonetheless "disposed" to publish.
A Boy's Will. He'd left boyhood after all.

2.

As a boy might skip a stone across a pond,
skim over fifty-one Octobers, to
the President with the winning smile. He'll fall
in less than one month's time in the Dallas sun.

He comes to return the favor of a white-
maned legend, lionized past recognition.
Once, squinting in the glare, fumbling with pages
that seemed on fire, the poet had declaimed
by heart (though he misspoke the young man's name)
a poem to inaugurate The New Frontier.
Robert Frost is dead; a library in his honor
at Amherst College today is dedicated.
"He knew the midnight as well as the high noon,"
Kennedy says. And now the library shelves
behind him will begin to accrete their proof.
Shoulder to shoulder, books file in like soldiers
to settle the literary territory
of one who has been seen as saint and monster.

One story goes back to Derry, New Hampshire, years
before England. Lesley was six or so.
In the middle of the night, she was awakened
by her father, who conducted her downstairs,
her feet cold on the floor. At the kitchen table
her mother wept, face hidden in her hands.
It was then that Lesley spotted the revolver.
"Take your choice," Frost said, as he waved the thing
between himself and Elinor — a less bracing
alternative than a poem unwritten yet
would give between two roads in a yellow wood.
"Before morning," he warned, "one of us will be dead."

The child was returned to bed. And only after
she'd tucked him in the earth would her memory
be brought to light — or fixed, at least, in print.
Was it true? Or a vivid, fluttering scarf of nightmare?
It wrapped, somehow, around the family neck.
For it wasn't Lesley, but her brother Carol
who — whether or not the grisly tale was real —
rewrote it with his life. It was the ninth

of October, 1940; he was thirty-eight.
He'd kept his own boy, Prescott, up for hours
with talk of his failures as a poet-farmer;
of fears (but here the doctors would be wrong —
his wife lived on for more than fifty years)
that Lillian might not even last the night.
When Prescott drifted off, he took the shotgun
he'd bought for Lillian as a wedding gift
and went downstairs, before the sun could rise,
to turn it on himself.

                    Strange how in families
time seeps through all we do, so that the order
in which things happen seems to bow before
the dreamlike authority of metaphor.
Marjorie, the baby, dies in childbirth;
Elinor (who was "the unspoken half,"
Frost said, "of everything I ever wrote" —
if it wasn't true, one has no doubt he meant it)
is stricken at the heart while climbing stairs,
as if away from the scenes to come, when Carol
step by step descends flights of despair,
and Irma's mind unravels in and out
of the hospital. Time spirals to rearrange
events to show us something beyond change.

"Two things are sure," Carol's father had written
to Lillian in the midst of a world war
in which, he thought, a man might best have died
a soldier. "He was driven distracted by life
and he was perfectly brave." And yet he runs
his hand across more pages, as if to smooth
the mound of a new grave: Carol's mind
was one, he writes this time, with a "twist from childhood."
Think how, the year before, he'd raced through stop-signs:
his eyes veered "off the road ahead too often."

Now Frost is eighty-eight. He can see ahead.
Poet of chance and choice, who tossed a coin
but knew which side his bread was buttered on,
who said, "The most inalienable right of man
is to go to hell in his own way," here he is
in a hospital bed, a hell he hasn't made.
He has a letter from Lesley, who knows him for
the stubborn vanities and selfless gestures.
She knows, dear girl, the words to make him well,
if anything can make him well. She calls him
"Robert Coeur de Lion." Too weak to write,
he dictates a final letter back to her.
"You're something of a Lesley de Lion
yourself," he says, and he commends the children's
poems she's been working on. It's good
to have a way with the young. The old man
hasn't lost his knack, even in prose,
for giving the truth the grandeur of a cadence.
"I'd rather be taken for brave than anything else."

Frost in Miami

PETER SCHMITT

A quarter-mile off
the steady two-lane
and down a spongy
leaf-soft path, you reach

the plot he wintered
in his 70's,
a fairytale copse
lush with tendrilled shade,

two acres of choice
real estate he penned
"Pencil Pines," and twin,
tiny cottages,

much-weathered pink frame
and affixed with small
brass plates labeled *East*
and *West*. He quartered

in the half called *East*,
where some morning sun
might trickle past thick
forest-pulp. *West*, then,

was for guests, and though
you would be hard-pressed
to tell from outside
the difference (inside,

far fewer bookshelves
brace *West's* small fireplace),
to liken these like-
unminded hemi-

spheres to the mind's own,
said to be the homes
of "thought" and "feeling,"
is to suggest how

some men choose to live
in one, visiting
at times the other —
although Frost himself

would have fast dispelled
any notion aimed
at simplifying
the mind of a man.

He might have instead
found his analogue
in the dense tangle
growing overhead,

and choking the laced
gazebo spanning
the buildings, whose snarls
confirm suspicions

that the passageway —
and each dark cottage —
has been maintained clear
and free of clutter

only too rarely
since his departure.

Now He Knows All There Is to Know. Now He Is Acquainted with the Day and Night

DELMORE SCHWARTZ

Robert Frost, 1875–1963

Whose wood this is I think I know:
He made it sacred long ago:
He will expect me, far or near
To watch that wood immense with snow.

That famous horse must feel great fear
Now that his noble rider's no longer here:
He gives his harness bells to rhyme
 — Perhaps he will be back, in time?

All woulds were promises he kept
Throughout the night when others slept:
Now that he knows all that he did not know,
His wood is holy, and full of snow,
and all the beauty he made holy long long ago
In Boston, London, Washington,
And once by the Pacific and once in Moscow:
  and now, and now
   upon the fabulous blue river ever
   or singing from a great white bough

And wherever America is, now as before,
  and now as long, long ago
He sleeps and wakes forever more!

   "O what a metaphysical victory
   The first day and night of death must be!"

Frost to Skellings,

EDMUND SKELLINGS

Skellings to Frost, it's difficult
Across this dark. I remember, of all things,
Your tie, conservative, with a little pattern,
Tight about the neck of a boiled shirt
Sharp with starch. Everything matched.
And your thin white hair combed forward
In a residue of vanity. That night
You couldn't eat before the reading,
But got down some egg custard.
We had our picture taken. The bright
Flash burnt your old eyes and they watered.
Then you leant to my ear and whispered,
As if it were the inside of your soul,
"The bastards are killing me." Oh Robert,
I went on after you died, but never
Righted a wrong. It's been a long time
Since you took my arm and mumbled almost
Under your breath, "It's a big step."

Frost

FLOYD SKLOOT

Wizened, spoiling for a fight, Frost is here
again. I have tried adjusting my pain
medication and sleep schedule, but still
he comes back to wander these woods like wind
stirring the Douglas fir. There is a gleam
of cold light where he stops and squats to track
the cries of naked oak that lean against
a surge of squalls.
             I hear him rhyming oak
with choke, then smoke and cloak as he looks down
into the valley. It will grow slowly
visible with the lifting of morning
mist and he will allow himself a small
smile. Spoke. Broke.
              Finally he turns to me,
lifting his chin to indicate the rough
grove at my back. "I see you lost your bees."
I nod as though I always speak with ghosts.
"They were gone before I got here."
                  Frost first
showed up with late September's heavy rain,
a creature of the equinox, I thought,
till I got a closer look. He follows
his own timetable like the pack of deer
that comes and goes now hunting season has
ended.
     "You need some chickens," he whispers.
"Good layers kept me and mine alive through
lean years." He leads me straight uphill. Baroque.
Folk. Roanoke. "Awoke," I say and he
stops dead to let me know who makes the rules.

Then his face unfolds, thawing as he seems
to grow young before my eyes. "Like your cane,"
he says, and winks when he adds "don't tell me:
Hazel from Rapallo in honor of
Ezra Pound." He shakes his shaggy head. Yoke.
Hoax. "They let him go when I told them to."

Because I have been reading Freud I know
this is the key. First illness, then prison,
then being freed by Frost. Wish-fulfillment,
the heart of every dream. He makes his way
toward a pile of pine and points to the axe.
Stroke. Soak. "Running low." I turn to find him
drifting west with the sun and well beyond
reach of my voice. "There is more seasoning
behind the gazebo," I tell thin air
and watch another morning shape itself
around the twist of winter on the wind.

Near Frost's Grave

DAVE SMITH

Rain in gray streaks thickens the beard of summer
in this Vermont valley, hiding the Revolution's
slabbed fieldstone, the broken-off family trees
volleys of wind hurl down at last to a man's spent
length in the secret weeds and moss-clefts. Filling
a farmhouse window the man rubs his unshaven face,
a soldier, perhaps, outflanked, wanting his life,
soaked with hunger and fear. He tries to remember.
The spatter of so much water makes him violent
with love of some lonely ground. He wants to take
the path visible through unmown hay, debouching
on wooded stillness past limbs snapping like snipers.
This much we think we can see, waiting out the rain.
We imagine he is thinking of his life in no-time.
Will I die in this meadow? We know he will fall,
someone shouting to hurry, run, and are amused by
a feather of smoke like flesh-char of a man's leg
where a doctor grunts. The soldier's face deadens.
A spruce points upward like an oil-sodden torch,
but to him flameless as God. He thinks rain means
he can't hear or see God, who commands him to look.
That is why he has faced a distant trunk, its crown
enormous and malignant with age, sees it thrashed
by the gusts, and sees the goldfinches thrown out
like yellow words at the storm, hopeless, then each
returned as if summoned, lodged anew in darkness,
their brilliance scarring the air raw as a logic.
Long he stands, listens, as if to drift as they do,
with no thought anyone may be watching, then bolts,
grateful for the rain washing his steps from earth.

Burial Code

LAUREL SMITH

> *The nearest friends can go*
> *With anyone to death, comes so far short*
> *They might as well not try to go at all.*
> — Frost, "Home Burial"

He did not want to be buried, you say.
Frail and thin in those last months,
he made a heavy weight,
unbelievably so
at the cemetery. You said

you feared that the six of you could not bear him;
Randy's back was bad, Ford and Billy
wearing nice shoes when they needed boots.
The wind was against you and icy rain stung your eyes.
But most of all, he did not want this final rest.
Not yet anyway, not yet.

Lying awake in this cold farmhouse
I read the story differently:

The dead must find
a new language, something
to be relayed and understood
as weight, not words.
Prepared or not, you have taken
the first test. Your
muscles know how to listen.
The next test is harder:
to convey this grammar to the arms
and back of another set of bearers.

Not yet, not yet.

Robert Frost: The Road Taken

WILLIAM JAY SMITH

The poet stopped on the edge of night,
 And the road through dark wound on.
Black trees arose; the wind was still;
Blind skeletal walls inched over the hill
 In the mole-gray dawn.

He thought of the way by which he had come,
 Mastered through long years —
Tangles of form and substance, dense
Thickets past which with experience
 A writer steers.

He gazed beyond the familiar night
 On the reasons reason curbs —
Adjectives which say too little,
Adverbs that flare, or with dust settle
 On shining verbs.

A dim house ahead, a journey completed,
 Out of darkness, dawn.
The blind walls move: his words awaken
Here on the page; and the road taken
 Winds on.

Frost

LAURENCE SNYDAL

You had a country touch, a Yankee air.
New England suited you. You wore, you swung
Its birches down to earth when you were young,
The silver birches that would shiver where
Death stopped his sleigh beside a snowy wood.
You paved a pathway with your gravel voice.
Dry as dirt, it measured memory and choice.
You spoke of tramps, witches. We understood.
We were the subjects of each cunning phrase.
The tattered patterns of a melting snow
Could show us how to be and where to go,
A way to wander through our everydays.
From the stone fence where apple trees begin,
Back to the home where they must take us in.

Robert Frost's Books, Ripton, Vermont, 1980

JOHN SOKOL

For Shelly (1940–1984)

Remember that day we found his books?
We had driven twelve hours from Ohio

to visit Bette and Joe in Vermont. We were
tourists — there, in Ripton — so, naturally,

we made our pilgrimage to Robert Frost's
cabin. Deer-hunting season had just begun,

and as we trudged through the white woods,
gunshots hammered the air and shook snow

from the branches of birches and sugar maples.
We were cold, and in love, and worried that

we might be mistaken for deer in our brown
coats. It was thrush-hour and a few crows cawed

in the treetops. As we approached the great poet's
cabin, you rephrased lines from his poems:

The woods are lovely, dark, and dangerous
So let's make promises we can keep,
And not get shot before we sleep.

When we reached his cabin, we were amazed
to find the door unlocked. We were timid

about going in: sacrilege, disrespect, and such.
But, "Oh, why not?" When we went inside,

we kissed behind the door, then laughed,
knowing we were thinking the same thing.

We closed the door and walked across
the pine-plank floor as though we were stepping

on hallowed ground. You stood quietly in
the middle of the room. You stared at the dusty

rocking chair, smiled, then looked at me. "Maybe,"
our faces said. I put my arms around you as we

stared at the single bed: iron; no mattress; just
springs. Then, we looked over at the wall

with the only window, and a view of the
Green Mountains. Two smiles made it unanimous.

But, then, we saw that crate at the foot of the bed;
a well-made pine box, labeled: Robert Frost's Books.

We lifted the lid and wondered who was in charge
of watching this historical cabin; of caring for

these precious books in a box. What ever happened
to ars longa, vita brevis? We couldn't believe

Frost's personal books were just sitting there
for some hunter to use as toilet paper or kindling:

Confucius, Herodotus, Horace, Tennyson,
Lucretius, Byron and Keats. Books on Vermont and

New Hampshire, wolves and wildlife: in a box,
on that cold, cabin floor. Somehow, we saw

nothing wrong with the idea of making
love in his cabin; but not in front of his books.

We left the books as we found them, replaced
the lid of the crate and closed the door of the cabin

when we left. "I wish we hadn't found his books,"
you said — four years later — when you were dying

of cancer; drowning in your own fluids, in my arms.
"I wish we had made love in his cabin, instead.

I'd take that memory with me, now." "I know,"
I said. "I wish we hadn't found them, either."

And, now, everyone will have to forgive me
for this, but I'd rather Robert Frost turn over
in his grave than not pay homage to you in yours:

I shall be telling this with a sigh
Somewhere ages and ages hence:
Two roads diverged in a wood, and you and I —
We took the one less traveled by,
And, in the end, that never made a difference.

Worse

J. R. SOLONCHE

One could do worse than be a swinger of birches.

For example, one could be a slinger of burgers at McDonald's.
Or one could be a bringer of frivolous lawsuits.
Or one could be a flinger of gossipy dirt for *The New York Post*.

Or one could be a singer of inane songs on MTV for pre-teens.
Or one could be a clinger of apron strings.
Or one could be a dead-ringer for one of the FBI's *Ten Most Wanted*.

Or one could be a hunch-backed ringer of French church bells.
Or one could be a second-stringer on a last place minor league baseball team.
Or one could be a stringer for a newspaper in the sticks.

Or one could be a finger man for the mafia.
Or one could be a dinger of car fenders in the parking lot of Wal-Mart.
Or one could be a left-winger for a last place minor league hockey team.

Or one could be a right-winger of any country's politics.
Or one could be a jingler of idiotic jingles on the radio for pre-teens.
Or one could be a malingerer.

At the Robert Frost Memorial

WILLIAM STAFFORD

We stand on marble here, the way he stood,
where trees grab hold and hills behind them rear,
and hesitate — a million years.

They move, though, and his family moved, along
the brook, out of the way — denim shapes,
and organdy, daughter, wife, and son.
They whittled whistles here that matched the birds,
more songs than the one whose reputation in cement enforces us.

Not marks on marble, but marble itself, will stay:
Let's pray our families will interrupt,
be brave enough to stand up to us — that
what there is to say of how we lived, our children say.

Fae

TIMOTHY STEELE

I bring Fae flowers. When I cross the street,
She meets and gives me lemons from her tree.
As if competitors in a Grand Prix,
The cars that speed past threaten to defeat
The sharing of our gardens and our labors.
Their automotive moral seems to be
That hell-for-leather traffic makes good neighbors.

Ten years a widow, standing at her gate,
She speaks of friends, her cat's trip to the vet,
A grandchild's struggle with the alphabet.
I conversationally reciprocate
With talk of work at school, not deep, not meaty.
Before I leave we study and regret
Her alley's newest samples of graffiti.

Then back across with caution: to enjoy
Fae's lemons, it's essential I survive
Lemons that fellow-Angelenos drive.
She's eighty-two; at forty, I'm a boy.
She waves goodbye to me with her bouquet.
This place was beanfields back in '35
When she moved with her husband to L.A.

Answering Robert Frost

FELIX STEFANILE

For Spencer Brown

The question that he frames in all but words
is what to make of a diminished thing.

Some things are best unsaid, and best unheard;
not even tattle-tale's a pretty bird,
but here's one now, that cardinal again.
He must proclaim himself. There are no flowers,
the land is bare, but he makes up for ten,
say cardinal flowers from the summer past.
The weather's threatening; we've had snow-showers,
and biting wind in heavy overcast.
The radio keeps bragging about the fall
in temperature; he won't shut up at all.
He may be saying this is for the birds,
and he's an omen. Furies liked to sing.
He may be telling us in his own words,
"If Rage is all that's left, Rage is a pleasant thing."

The Sun Used to Shine

EDWARD THOMAS

The sun used to shine while we two walked
Slowly together, paused and started
Again, and sometimes mused, sometimes talked
As either pleased, and cheerfully parted

Each night. We never disagreed
Which gate to rest on. The to be
And the late past we gave small heed.
We turned from men or poetry

To rumours of the war remote
Only till both stood disinclined
For aught but the yellow flavorous coat
Of an apple wasps had undermined:

Or a sentry of dark betonies,
The stateliest of small flowers on earth,
At the forest verge: or crocuses
Pale purple as if they had their birth

In sunless Hades fields. The war
Came back to mind with the moonrise
Which soldiers in the east afar
Beheld then. Nevertheless, our eyes

Could as well imagine the Crusades
Or Caesar's battles. Everything
To faintness like those rumours fades —
Like the brook's water glittering

Under the moonlight — like those walks
Now — like us two that took them, and
The fallen apples, all the talks
And silences — like memory's sand

When the tide covers it late or soon,
And other men through other flowers
In those fields under the same moon
Go talking and have easy hours.

Living at the Frost Place

SUE ELLEN THOMPSON

The day my daughter leaves for California,
I'm three hundred miles north
in the Franconia, New Hampshire, farmhouse
where Robert Frost lived with his wife
and four young children. I don't call
to tell her to pack vitamins and sunblock,
I don't ask what airline or what flight she's on.
She's old enough to make her way
from one end of the continent to another.

I spend the morning writing
at my makeshift summer desk on the verandah,
Mount Lafayette a hazy blue reminder
of the obstacles that pierce the sky at intervals
from here to the Sierras. The Morris chair
Frost sat in when he wrote the great poems
of his middle years stands brooding
in the parlor, flanked by manuscripts
and letters in glass cases — stern reminders
that I've reached the point in life where work
must come before the fretful agitations of a parent.

I take the silkscreened print she made me
for my birthday — an abstract latticework
in red and black like synapses, or the mysteries
of blood — down from the mantel and replace it
with a photo of the poet on the peak of Lafayette
surrounded by his children: disapproving
Lesley; Marjorie, who died of complications
following childbirth; Carol, melancholy boy
who shot himself; Irma, terrified
of men, who went insane.

For Christine at the Frost Farm

DANIEL TOBIN

Ripton, Vermont

The master's cabin's overrun by mice
or something bigger that's dragged your store
of fresh-ground coffee across the floor
as though it were the poet's teasing trace

of something dark and deep that had gotten in
from the woods outside, leaving its small scats
on the linen. You say you'll make the best
of it, long-distance, on the phone.

Hearing you, I find myself fending away
my own slinking pest inside, the creature
cringing in solitude's bleak nest; or worse,
that shadow transfigured by the urge to save,

and purge all impediment to your hunger —
words laid down like a bright trail from your life.
Follow it farther than you can see now, love,
awake all night, spying the miles to go.

Happiness

MICHAEL VAN WALLEGHEN

Weep for what little things could make them glad.
— *Robert Frost, "Directive"*

Melvin,
      the large collie
who lives in the red house
at the end of my daily run
is happy,
      happy to see me
even now,
      in February —
a month of low skies
and slowly melting snow.

His yard
      has turned almost
entirely to mud —
            but so what?

Today,
      as if to please me,
he has torn apart
            and scattered
everywhere
      a yellow plastic bucket
the color of forsythia
or daffodils . . .

      And now,
in a transport
            of cross-eyed
muddy ecstasy,

he has placed
his filthy two front paws
together
    on the top pipe
of his sagging cyclone fence —

drooling a little,
       his tail
wagging furiously,
       until finally,
as if I were God's angel himself —

fulgent,
    blinding,
       aflame
with news of the Resurrection,
I give him a biscuit
       instead.

Which is fine with Melvin —
who is wise,
    by whole epochs
of evolution,
    beyond his years.

Take
    what you can get,
that's his motto . . .

    And really,
apropos of bliss,
    happiness
and the true rapture,
    what saint
could tell us half as much?

Even as he drops
    back down

into the cold
  dog-shit muck
he'll have to live in
  every day
for weeks on end perhaps
unless it freezes . . .

whining now,
 dancing
nervously
 as I turn away
again,
  to leave him there

the same today
  as yesterday —

one of the truly wretched
of this earth
 whose happiness
is almost more
  than I can bear.

The Wall between Us

MARK VINZ

He moves in darkness as it seems to me.
— Robert Frost

Late in the afternoon of Halloween
my new neighbor stops by to introduce
himself at the front door. At first I think
it must be an early trick-or-treater —
a young father with his small son in tow,
both staring at our grinning jack o'lantern
and then the bowl of brightly-wrapped candy.
Take some, I say, but the father says no,
sharply — they have their own candy at home,
and besides, they don't participate in
godless rituals. He's simply here to
give me notice he's putting up a fence
between our two backyards — mostly for dogs,
he says, two Labradors who'll need the space.
But not to worry about any noise —
they'll be fitted with special collars
which will shock them if they dare to bark.
When I joke about the line *good fences*
make good neighbors, he simply stares, then says
the Lord has blessed him with a growing family.

True to his word, a six-foot high board fence
goes up in days, followed by the dogs,
so strangely silent in their circling
and endlessly alone — I can't help feeling
glad weeks later when I hear that one of them
escaped, and gladder still to find out that
my neighbor bought the house to fix it up

for quick resale. He'll be gone by spring —
but for his pamphlets on finding the Lord,
a fence that casts long shadows in the yards,
and a small boy's eyes, darting hopelessly
from a bowl of candy to his father's frown.

The Kindness of Abishag

DAVI WALDERS

The witch that came (the withered hag) . . .
Was once the beauty Abishag
—Robert Frost, "Provide, Provide"

Imagine my offense to see "witch," "hag,"
"pail and rag" attached to me. Such words
do violence to my story. Oh, they rhyme

amusingly with my name, but remember who
I was and my time. Young, with wit and charm.
The king was withered, cold. I was warm

enough for two, held him in my arms
but he could not last. What battles
in that court! Absolom, then Adonijah.

He made such a scene before the queen
begging for my hand when he wanted
only to be king. I tried to tell him

I was no stepping stone to the crown.
But Adonijah? Listen? Never. Somebody
killed him. I returned to Shunem, built

a home, lived in peace. Elisha came often
as he wandered the land. I added a room,
a small space for him to stay. Why not

be kind when one can? He said I would have
a child. How odd, I thought, but it was true.
A healthy boy, until he suddenly fell ill

and died. I was desperate trying to revive
him. I ran in search of Elisha. Had I been
deceived? He lay upon the child, warmed

him and prayed until, just as suddenly
as he died, my son sneezed himself seven
times awake. A fit of sneezing? A miracle,

a gift of warmth? Odd again, but true.
So remember Abishag (not as a hag) but
friend to prophets, kings, who early

learned when one has youth, warmth,
food, a bed, it's best to give,
not horde and hide. Provide, provide.

On the Road to Homer Noble Farm

KIM WALLER

Hey, green! going down the road in Ripton,
going to visit the old man once,
up to my knees in jewelweed
    as trucks gear down passing up-mountain
and me in the dust scuffing up mica
    in high August, taking my time
on the log bridge (wood rot
    and hot of tar) where Brandywine Brook
switches sides and goes under.

And me going down by the church steps
    where daylilies bunch: Hallelujah
in yellow mouths — *invited*
    with mountains around me in green dives
and the sky that day from shoulder to shoulder
    mine — *to come on down*
to the farm, he said, *and bring poems.*
    Hey tamarack fur! Poplar in jitters!
     Bright stones!

Robert Frost at the Net

DANEEN WARDROP

Forty-love:
From the deuce court Frost serves for the match,
the figure a poem makes, arching, a swan of arms converging
                    and a smash —
          angle and restitution and molecules.
His opponent, the department chair, has heard it
rumored that he must let Frost win —
but not tank so much as to seem coddling —
to assure a good reading tonight.
With a close win, a great reading.

Forty-fifteen:
Before Frost hits he sees the ball's seam curve a figure eight
that doesn't cross itself. Each game a conversion.
              An ant lugs its shadow across the end T.
          He thinks, Those who would be so foolish as to keep score with God.
He has followed his footprints from every
ice-crusted back forty he's ever trod,
he's wanted to come home since love opened
the first set two hours ago.

Forty-thirty:
Department chair worries:
was the backhand this time supercilious? the volley bravura?
then snaps a cross-court shot
that means it.
They are mailing the ball to each other,
express now. The chair has forgotten he needs to lose,
only remembers that it needs to be close.

Deuce:
Sweat, a profound caesura.
A half-volley saves the point.

Ad-in:

A rhythm awaits.
Flagrant forsythia by the water fountain.
Come summer trees will elaborate on their bios.
First serve, bounce and clank — long — against chain link.
Second serve, feckless — cuts top of the net,
makes popped corn of the ball,
drops back in server's court.
Double fault anger.
The net forgets itself.

Deuce again:

World without leverage. Department chair forgets his poetry,
returns the chary serve with a lob to the back line,
slim as a promise,
but on the line.

Ad-out:

Frost tastes on his tongue blood
from the lurch, or water full of minerals
as if a word with too many syllables.
First serve he cracks, in, and both players have reason
to be patient with the point. They play it as if a joint
conspiracy, and in truth
it's been in play since the beginning
of enjambment. But the chair
betrays the play:
a swing and it's game,

and the match is only half-way
through the afternoon.
Frost towels his arms and face.

He will not write a poem today.

Making Love at the Frost Place

MICHAEL WATERS

Franconia, NH

His name — **R. Frost** — writ large in bold strokes on the mailbox,
the village luminary
hunkers in wraithlike presence over his writing desk,
or shuffles in slippers past
the open hearth, milky hair and graphite-needled face
such familiar portraiture
we can't not see him rage as we clutch each other, not
hear him groan as we commence
late August lovemaking during such perishable
tenancy, until we learn
again, *night falling fast*, what school children flame to know:
the common language that breathes
autumn into *apples*, winter into *sleep* and *snow*.

On Not Finding Frost's Grave in the Dark

BRUCE WEIGL

So close I felt a rift in the air
of the kind when a soul tries to call,
but I could not go to his grave.
I'd had enough with the dead,
so I drank something sweet and bitter
among beautiful women
and their stories no one wanted to hear,
and I danced with a boy named Mohammed
in the meadow, angels,
whom I could not distinguish from our bodies,
cutting through what
fleshy light they could find.

Ghost Frost

ROGER WEINGARTEN

All out of doors looked darkly in at him
— *Robert Frost, "An Old Man's Winter Night"*

Pale orchid sunrise snaking through fog,
Hell of summer frost on tomato leaf.
An oriole, all compressed fear, lights near a grove of yellow birch

Not many yards from the glow of farmer Tabor's
Twist of tobacco pinched between his teeth, that, in silent acquiescence, says,
Ok, let's call a six pack breakfast or consign the day to the feeble

Moon of morning, if you get my drift. A rusted metal sheet falling through the
    rafters
Of Tabor's barn startles store-bought cheaters off his capillary-ruined nose that
Fills half his face, the other half trying not to fix on the phantom of a

Fidgety and distracted ex, who penned sonnets to fiddlehead jam cooling on the
    sill.
Remember, she's the one who left him in a borrowed jacket and clip-on tie. That
Old farmer who sleeps it off in his overalls in a stall, hay-strewn, under bats and
    barn

Swallows diving, not for animal warmth but for a self-amused, self-inflicted
Tit for tat. That frost-burned old man feeling around for his glasses in the dirt.

After All

THEODORE WEISS

Robert Frost, expatiating
on his work, confessed to David Daiches
that if, after the first few lines,
a poem faltered, lost its wits,
grew skittish, he let it go.

So he got no more than the idea
of it out into the open, into another
man's mind (now mine). That way
it was, after all, recorded how,
going out to work

                  in the woods,
he often saw more — the eye freed —
in feather, leaf, and little creature
than going into it with sight
in mind.

         Later, thanking Daiches
for writing about the Latin writers
plainly behind him (a fact most critics
failed to see), Frost explained that he
had started studying Latin

                  long ago
and with a schoolmarm in no way
interested in the poetry but only
the Roman road-like grammar, and he
for the longest time resented her.

But now he saw it may have been
for the best: not a mad beeline
to the honey but laying out the slow,
pedestrian cobbles block by block,

then footing it uphill,
                    down, letting
wayside flowers, butterflies, and birds
waft out their fragrant stuff, a crazy
traffic run athwart the wars, the work-
aday, the slogging legionnaires.

Traveling with Cats on a Snowy Evening

GAIL WHITE

I've no idea whose woods these are,
But I'm not getting very far
From Albany to NYC
With two cats yowling in my car.

These dratted cats must think it queer
To stop without a sandbox near,
But listen, guys, I'm twice your size,
so use the woods or else, you hear?

They give their big round eyes a blink
To ask each other what they think,
And I can tell they'll make life hell
And plan on driving me to drink.

The woods are lovely, dark, and deep.
The car is slowing to a creep.
Why did I try to cross NY?
I'm breathing cat hairs in my sleep.

Seed Leaves

RICHARD WILBUR

Homage to R. F.

Here something stubborn comes,
Dislodging the earth crumbs
And making crusty rubble.
It comes up bending double,
And looks like a green staple.
It could be seedling maple,
Or artichoke, or bean.
That remains to be seen.

Forced to make choice of ends,
The stalk in time unbends,
Shakes off the seed-case, heaves
Aloft, and spreads two leaves
Which still display no sure
And special signature.
Toothless and fat, they keep
The oval form of sleep.

This plant would like to grow
And yet be embryo;
Increase, and yet escape
The doom of taking shape;
Be vaguely vast, and climb
To the tip end of time
With all of space to fill,
Like boundless Igdrasil
That has the stars for fruit.

But something at the root
More urgent than that urge
Bids two true leaves emerge,
And now the plant, resigned
To being self-defined
Before it can commerce
With the great universe,
Takes aim at all the sky
And starts to ramify.

Home: After a Poem by Frost

STEVE WILSON

Down from the stairs:
they'd done with each other.
He sat at the kitchen table,

lost in the light from
the window — light broken by
green curtains. Some steps away,

a clock insisted upon
each second that slipped through
another click of its gears.

She brushed away the wrinkles
in her dress. She found herself
staring where the child had been,

remembering time can be so exacting
in loss — how it measures us
within its own persistent solitudes.

Notes on Contributors

Joe Aimone teaches creative writing, literature, and technical writing at Santa Clara University in California.

Tony Barnstone is the author of *Impure*, a collection of poems, and the editor of *Out of the Howling Storm: The New Chinese Poetry*; *Laughing Lost in the Mountains: Selected Poems of Wang Wei*; *The Art of Writing: Techniques of the Chinese Masters*; and *The Anchor Book of Chinese Poetry*. He teaches at Whittier College in California.

Willis Barnstone is the author of more than forty-five collections of poetry, scholarship, translations, and memoir, including *Life Watch*; *Algebra of Night: New and Selected Poems, 1948–1998*; *The Secret Reader: 501 Sonnets*; *We Jews and Blacks*; *With Borges on an Ordinary Evening in Buenos Aires*; *Sunday Morning in Fascist Spain*; *The Poetics of Translation*; and, most recently, *Border of a Dream: Selected Poems of Antonio Machado*. His literary translation of the New Testament is entitled *The New Covenant* (vol. 1: *The Four Gospels and the Apocalypse*). He is distinguished professor of comparative literature, Spanish, and east Asian cultures at Indiana University.

Marvin Bell divides his time among Iowa City, Iowa; Sag Harbor, New York; and Port Townsend, Washington. Among his eighteen collections of poems are *Rampant*; *Nightworks: Poems 1962–2000*; *The Book of the Dead Man*; and *Ardor*. He is Flannery O'Connor Professor of Letters at the University of Iowa, where he has taught for more than three decades. In April 2002, he was appointed to a second term as Iowa's poet laureate.

Wendell Berry is the author of more than thirty books of poetry, essays, novels, and short stories. His collections of poetry include *The Selected Poems of Wendell Berry*; *A Timbered Choir: The Sabbath Poems 1979–1997*; *Entries: Poems*; *Traveling at Home*; *Collected Poems 1957–1982*; and *Clearing*. His novels and short fiction include *That Distant Land*, *Jayber Crow*, *A World Lost*, *Remembering*, and *The Memory of Old Jack*. Berry is also the author of prose collections including *Another Turn of the Crank*; *Sex, Economy, Freedom, & Community*; *Standing on Earth:*

Selected Essays; *The Unsettling of America: Culture and Agriculture*; and *A Continuous Harmony: Essays Cultural and Agricultural*. He has taught at New York University and at the University of Kentucky. Among his honors and awards are fellowships from the Guggenheim and Rockefeller foundations, a Lannan Foundation award, and a grant from the National Endowment for the Arts. He lives on a farm in Port Royal, Kentucky.

Robert Bly's many books of poems include *Silence in the Snowy Fields*, *The Light Around the Body* — winner of the National Book Award — and, most recently, *The Night Abraham Called to the Stars* and *Eating the Honey of Words: New and Selected Poems*. Recent collections of translations include *The Winged Energy of Delight: Selected Translations*; *The Half-Finished Heaven: The Best Poems of Tomas Tranströmer*; and *The Lightening Should Have Fallen on Ghalib* (with Sunil Dutta). His essays have been collected in *Iron John*, *The Sibling Society*, *The Maiden King* (with Marion Woodman), and *American Poetry: Wildness and Domesticity*.

Alec Bond, author of *Poems for an Only Daughter*, *North of Sioux Falls*, and *Phoebus Lane*, a posthumous collection, was for many years chair of the English department at Southwest State University in Marshall, Minnesota. He died in 1986.

N. M. Brewka has been a professional writer for more than thirty years. Her poems have appeared in many magazines and anthologies. She is also a playwright. She lives in Beverly, Massachusetts.

Kim Bridgford directs the writing program at Fairfield University, where she is a professor of English and editor of *Dogwood*. In 1994, she was named Connecticut Professor of the Year by the Carnegie Foundation for the Advancement of Teaching. Her collections of poems include *Undone* and *Eden's Gift*, a letterpress edition of poems.

Gwendolyn Brooks published her first poem when she was thirteen years old. In the 1930s, she met James Weldon Johnson and Langston Hughes, who encouraged her to read modern poetry and to write. Her first collection of poems, *A Street in Bronzeville,* was published in 1945. Her second collection, *Annie Allen,* won the Pulitzer Prize in 1949. Among her many collections of poems are *Children Coming Home, Blacks, To*

Disembark, The Near-Johannesburg Boy and Other Poems, *Riot*, *The Bean Eaters*, *Selected Poems*, *The Wall*, and *In the Mecca*. Brooks's collections of poems for children include *Bronzeville Boys and Girls* and *We Real Cool*. *Report from Part One* is an autobiographical collection of personal memoirs, interviews, and letters. She is also the author of a novel, *Maud Martha*. She died in 2000.

Hayden Carruth is the author or editor of thirty-one books, including a novel, four books of criticism, and two anthologies. His most recent collections of poetry include *Doctor Jazz*; *Collected Shorter Poems, 1946–1991*, awarded the National Book Critics Circle Award; and *Scrambled Eggs and Whiskey*, which won the National Book Award for poetry. He has been editor of *Poetry* and poetry editor of *Harper's*. After many years of teaching in the Graduate Creative Writing Program at Syracuse University, he retired in 1994. He continues to live and write in upstate New York.

Dan Chiasson is the author of *The Afterlife of Objects*. He teaches at SUNY — Stony Brook, where he directs the Poetry Center.

Bruce Cohen is director of the Counseling Program for Intercollegiate Athletics at the University of Connecticut. His poems have appeared in numerous literary journals.

Wyn Cooper is the author of *Postcards from the Interior*, *The Country Here Below* (from which two poems were made into songs by Sheryl Crow, including "All I Want to Do"), *The Way Back*, and *Secret Address*. Prior to turning to full-time writing in 1996, he taught at Bennington and Marlboro colleges. With Madison Smart Bell, he has recorded the CD *Forty Words for Fear*. He lives in Vermont.

Robert Cooperman is the author of *Petitions for Immortality: Scenes from the Life of John Keats*; *The Widow's Burden*; *A Tale of the Grateful Dead*; *In The Colorado Gold Fever Mountains*, recipient of the Colorado Book Award for poetry in 2000; and *In the Household of Percy Bysshe Shelley*. He lives in Denver, Colorado.

Nina Corwin is a psychotherapist, the author of *Conversations with Friendly Demons and Tainted Saints*, and coeditor of *Inhabiting the Body: A Collection of Poetry and Art By Women*. She lives in Chicago.

Todd Davis teaches creative writing and literature at Penn State University–Altoona. He is the author of *Ripe*, a collection of poems.

Peter Davison is the author of eleven books of poetry, most recently *The Poems of Peter Davison* and *Breathing Room*, recipient of the 2000 Massachusetts Book Award. He is also the author of *The Faded Smile: Poets in Boston, from Robert Frost to Robert Lowell to Sylvia Plath, 1955–1960* and poetry editor of the *Atlantic Monthly*. He died in 2005.

Madeline DeFrees is the author of seven collections of poetry, most recently *Blue Dusk: New and Selected Poems, 1951–2001*, recipient of the Lemore Marshall Prize from the Academy of American Poets, a Washington Book Award, and the first annual Denise Levertov Award sponsored by *Image: A Journal of the Arts and Religion*. She is also the author of two prose memoirs. She lives in Seattle, Washington.

George Drew's collections of poems include *Toads in a Poisoned Tank* and a chapbook, *So Many Bones (Poems of Russia)*, in a bilingual edition. In June 2004, he was a guest poet at the Conference on Teaching and Poetry at the Frost Place. He lives in Poestenkill, New York.

Richard Eberhart's first book of poetry, *A Bravery of Earth*, was published in 1931, the same year Robert Frost won his second Pulitzer Prize for his *Collected Poems*. Since then, he has published many collections of poems, including *Selected Poems*, recipient of the 1966 Pulitzer Prize; *The Long Reach: New and Uncollected Poems, 1948–1984*; *New and Selected Poems: 1930–1990*; *Maine Poems*; and *Collected Poems 1930–1986*, recipient of the National Book Award. He received the Frost Medal from the Poetry Society of America, and in 1962, he received the Bollingen Prize for Poetry, a year before Robert Frost received the same award.

Rhina P. Espaillat is the author of seven collections of poems, including *Playing at Stillness*; *The Shadow I Dress In*; *Where Horizons Go*, winner of the 1998 T. S. Eliot Prize; and *Rehearsing Absence*, winner of the 2001 Richard Wilbur Award. She lives in Newburyport, Massachusetts.

Dave Etter is the author of twenty-nine collections of poems, including *Alliance, Illinois*; *Live at the Silver Dollar*; *Selected Poems*; *Sunflower County*; *How High the Moon*; and most recently, *Looking for Sheena Easton*. He lives in Lanark, Illinois.

Annie Finch's books of poetry include *Eve*, *Calendars*, and *The Encyclopedia of Scotland*, as well as a translation of the complete poems of Louise Labe. She has also written, edited, or coedited books on poetry and poetics, including *The Ghost of Meter*; *An Exaltation of Forms: Contemporary Poets Celebrate the Diversity of Their Art*; and *The Body of Poetry*. She directs the Stonecoast MFA program at the University of Southern Maine.

Susan Firer is the author of four books of poetry, most recently *The Laugh We Make When We Fall*, winner of the Backwaters Prize, and *The Lives of the Saints and Everything*, winner of the Cleveland State Poetry Prize. She lives in Milwaukee, Wisconsin.

Robert Francis spent most of his life living and writing in and around Amherst, Massachusetts. Among his many collections of poems are *The Orb Weaver*; *Come Out into the Sun: Poems New and Selected*; and *Late Fire: New and Uncollected Poems*. *Pot Shots at Poetry* is a collection of his essays and criticism. He died in Amherst in 1980.

James Galvin is the author of six collections of poems, most recently *X* and *Resurrection Update: Collected Poems, 1975–1997*. He is also the author of a book of nonfiction, *The Meadow*, and a novel, *Fencing the Sky*. He divides his time between Iowa City, where he teaches at the University of Iowa Writers' Workshop, and his ranch near Tie Siding, Wyoming.

Wilfrid Wilson Gibson was a member of the Dymock Poets group that included Lascelles Abercrombie, Rupert Brooke, John Drinkwater, Robert Frost, and Edward Thomas. Shortly after the Frosts arrived in England in October of 1912, Frost met Gibson in London at Harold Monro's Poetry Bookshop, where Gibson rented a room above the shop. Gibson's poem "The First Meeting" recalls that time. Gibson, a popular poet in both England and the United States, was an early admirer of Frost's poetry. In March of 1914, at Gibson's urging, the Frosts left their Beaconsfield house west of London for a sixteenth century cottage further west in the scenic Dymock region in the Gloucestershire countryside, where they would become neighbors to Gibson and Abercrombie. Shortly thereafter, Frost wrote to a friend back in the U.S. that "Gibson is my best friend," but later their friendship was strained because of Gibson's less than flattering review of *North of Boston*. "The Golden Room" is Gibson's nostalgic recollection, written more than ten years after a June 1914 gathering of Abercrombie, Frost, Gibson, Thomas and their wives, and Brooke. When Frost returned to England in 1928, he and his wife visited the Gibsons. Gibson's poem "Reunion" recalls the event, and Gibson dedicated his next book, *Hazards*, to the Frosts. "The Golden Room" was published in the *Atlantic Monthly* in February 1926 and was collected in *The Best Poetry of 1926*. Gibson died in 1962, less than a year before Frost.

Gail Hosking Gilberg is the author of *Snake's Daughter: The Roads In and Out of War*, a prose memoir. Her poems and essays have appeared in numerous magazines and journals. She lives in Rochester, New York.

Michael S. Glaser teaches at St. Mary's College of Maryland and serves as a Poet-in-the-Schools for the Maryland State Arts Council. He is the author of three collections of poems: *A Lover's Eye*, *In the Men's Room and Other Poems*, and *Being a Father*.

David Graham was poet in residence at the Frost Place in Franconia, New Hampshire, in 1996, and has served on the faculty at the Frost Festival. His poems have appeared in six collections, including *Magic Shows*, *Second Wind*, and *Stutter Monk*. With Kate Sontag, he is coeditor of the essay anthology *After Confession: Poetry as Autobiography*. He is professor of English at Ripon College.

Thom Gunn, born in Gravesend, Kent, England, in 1929 and educated at Trinity College, Cambridge, moved to San Francisco in 1954, where he studied with Yvor Winters at Stanford University. He is the author of more than thirty books of poetry in the United States and Britain, including *Boss Cupid*; *Frontiers of Gossip*; *Collected Poems*; *The Man with Night Sweats*, recipient of the Lenore Marshall Poetry Prize; *Selected Poems 1950–1975*; and *My Sad Captains*. He has also written several collections of essays, including *The Occasions of Poetry*. He died on April 25, 2004, in his home in San Francisco.

Michael Heffernan is the author of seven books of poems, including, most recently, *The Night Breeze Off the Ocean*. His collection, *Love's Answer*, received the 1993 Iowa Poetry Prize. Since 1986, he has taught in the creative writing program at the University of Arkansas, Fayetteville.

William Heyen lives in Brockport, New York. A former Senior Fulbright Lecturer in American Literature in Germany, he recently edited *September 11, 2001: American Writers Respond*. Recent collections of his poems include *Shoah Train* and *The Rope*.

Larkin Higgins's poems and other writings have been published in numerous magazines and anthologies. A past artist-in-residence at Dorland Mountain Arts Colony, she lives in Los Angeles and teaches in Ventura County.

Edward J. Ingebretsen teaches in the English Department at Georgetown University, where he also directs the American Studies Program. He is the author of the critical study, *Robert Frost's Star in a Stone Boat: A Grammar of Belief*.

Richard Jackson is the author of four collections of poems: *Half Lives: Petrarchan Poems*; *Unauthorized Autobiography: New and Selected Poems*; *Alive All Day*; and *Heartwell,* winner of the 2001 Juniper Prize. He teaches at the University of Tennessee at Chattanooga and is on the staff of the Iowa Summer Writers Festival, the Vermont College MFA program, and the Prague Workshops.

Gray Jacobik's books include *Brave Disguises*, recipient of the 2001 Associated Writing Program Poetry Series Award; *The Surface of Last Scattering*, recipient of the 1999 X. J. Kennedy Prize; and *The Double Task*, recipient of the 1998 Juniper Prize. She is a member of the faculty of the Stonecoast MFA Program. She lives in Connecticut.

X. J. Kennedy's collections of poems include *The Lords of Misrule*, winner of the 2004 Poets' Prize; *Dark Horses*; and *Nude Descending a Staircase: Poems, Songs, A Ballad*. His textbooks, *An Introduction to Poetry* and *An Introduction to Fiction*, coedited with Dana Gioa, are among the most widely used texts in American colleges. With his wife, Dorothy, he has edited college writing textbooks and children's anthologies. He lives in Lexington, Massachusetts.

David Keplinger is the author of two collections of poetry, *The Clearing* and *The Rose Inside*. He has received fellowships from the National Endowment for the Arts and the Pennsylvania Council on the Arts. He directs the undergraduate creative writing program at the Colorado State University–Pueblo.

Galway Kinnell, a former MacArthur Fellow and State Poet of Vermont, is the author of twelve collections of poetry, including *Selected Poems*, winner of the Pulitzer Prize and the National Book Award in 1982. His most recent collection is *A New Selected Poems*. He lives in New York City and Vermont.

Kenneth Koch's many collections of poetry include the epic *Ko, or A Season on Earth*; *The Art of Love*; *New Addresses*, winner of the Phi Beta Kappa Poetry Award and a finalist for the National Book Award; *Straits*; *One Train* and *On the Great Atlantic Rainway: Selected Poems 1950–1988*, which together earned him the Bollingen Prize in 1995; *On the Edge*; *Days and Nights*; *Thank You*; and *Seasons on Earth*. He has also published *Making Your Own Days: The Pleasures of Reading and Writing Poetry*; *The Red Robins*, a novel; *Hotel Lambosa and Other Stories*; and several books on teaching children to write poetry, including *Wishes, Lies and Dreams* and *Rose, Where Did You Get That Red?* Koch lived in New York City, where he was professor of English at Columbia University. Koch died on July 6, 2002.

Tom Koontz directed the creative writing program at Ball State University in Muncie, Indiana, prior to his retirement in 2004. His chapbooks of poetry include *A Book of Charms*, *In Such a Light*, and *Rice Paper Sky*. He lives in Selma, Indiana, in the oldest house in Delaware County, with his wife, the painter Nina B. Marshall.

Norbert Krapf taught at Long Island University for thirty-four years, where he directed the C. W. Post Poetry Center. In 2004, he returned to his native Indiana, where he writes full time. He is the author of thirteen collections of poems, including *Somewhere in Southern Indiana*, *The Country I Come From*, and *Looking for God's Country*.

Maxine Kumin is the author of more than a dozen collections of poetry, including *Up Country: Poems of New England*, winner of the Pulitzer Prize in 1973. She has also written twenty books for children, four novels, and three collections of essays. She is the author of *Inside the Halo and Beyond*, a memoir, and *Always Beginning: Essays on a Life in Poetry*. She has served as consultant in poetry to the Library of Congress and as poet laureate of New Hampshire, and is a former chancellor of the Academy of American Poets. She lives in New Hampshire.

Sydney Lea, founder and for thirteen years editor of the *New England Review*, is the author of a novel, two collections of naturalist essays, and eight collections of poetry, including *Ghost Pain; Pursuit of a Wound,* a finalist for the 2001 Pulitzer Prize; *To the Bone: New and Selected Poems,* winner the 1997–1998 Poets' Prize; *Searching the Drowned Man; The Floating Candles;* and *The Blainville Testament.* He teaches in the graduate program at Dartmouth College.

David Lehman is the series editor of *The Best American Poetry,* which he launched in 1988. He is the author of five collections of poems, most recently *The Evening Sun* and *The Daily Mirror: A Journal in Poetry.* His books of criticism include *The Last Avant-Garde: The Making of the New York School of Poets,* named a "Book to Remember 1999" by the New York Public Library. Lehman also has edited such books as *Great American Prose Poems: From Poe to the Present; Ecstatic Occasions, Expedient Forms: 85 Leading Contemporary Poets Select and Comment on Their Poems; James Merrill: Essays in Criticism;* and *Beyond Amazement: New Essays on John Ashbery.* He teaches in the graduate writing programs at Bennington College and New School University. He lives in New York City.

Lyn Lifshin is the author of more than one hundred collections of poems, including most recently *When a Cat Dies; Another Woman Who Looks Like Me; Cold Comfort: Selected Poems;* and *Before It's Light.* She is also the editor of four anthologies of women's writing, including *Tangled Vines, Ariadne's Thread,* and *Lips Unleashed.* An award-winning documentary of her life is entitled *Lyn Lifshin, Not Made of Glass.* She lives in Virginia.

Rachel Loden's collections of poems include *Hotel Imperium* and a chapbook, *In the Graveyard of Fallen Monuments.* She lives in California.

Robert Lowell's many collections of poetry, prose, plays, and translations include *Lord Weary's Castle* (Pulitzer Prize, 1947), *Life Studies* (National Book Award, 1960), *Phaedra, Imitations, For the Union Dead, The Old Glory, Prometheus Bound, History, The Dolphin* (Pulitzer Prize, 1974),

Selected Poems, The Oresteia of Aeschylus, Collected Prose, and *Collected Poems.* He died in 1977.

Paul Marion is the author of several collections of poetry, most recently *Rosemont Stars: Selected Poems,* a bilingual edition (English/French), and the editor of *Atop an Underwood: Early Stories and Other Writings by Jack Kerouac.* He is coeditor of *The Bridge Review: Merrimack Valley Culture,* and online journal at the University of Massachusetts, Lowell, where he is the director of community relations.

David Mason is the author of *Arrivals, The Country I Remember, The Buried Houses, Land without Grief,* and *Small Elegies,* all collections of poems; and *The Poetry of Life and the Life of Poetry,* a collection of essays. With Mark Jarman he is coeditor of *Rebel Angels: 25 Poets of the New Formalism,* and with John Frederick Nims the 4th Edition of *Western Wind: An Introduction to Poetry.* He teaches at Colorado College.

William Matthews is the author of twelve collections of poems, including *Ruining the New Road, Flood, Blues If You Want, Selected Poems and Translations, After All,* and *Search Party: Collected Poems.* He received the National Book Critics Circle award in 1995 for *Time & Money: New Poems.* His essays and interviews are collected in *The Poetry Blues: Essays and Interviews* and *Curiosities.* At the time of his death in 1997, he was professor of English and director of the writing program at the City University of New York.

Sarah Katherine McCann earned her BA in English from Princeton and an MFA from the University of Iowa Writers' Workshop. As a Fulbright Scholar, she traveled to Greece to write and translate. Her collections of poetry are *Lettuce* and *Show Your Work.* Currently, she is editing a book of poetry by Robert Lax.

Peter Meinke has published twelve books of poems, most recently *Zinc Fingers* and *Liquid Paper: New and Selected Poems.* He holds the Darden Chair in Creative Writing at Old Dominion University in Norfolk, Virginia.

William Meredith is the author of nine books of poetry, including *Effort at Speech: New and Selected Poems,* for which he won the National Book Award in 1997; *Partial Accounts: New and Selected Poems,* which won the Pulitzer Prize in 1988; and *Love Letter from an Impossible Land,* which was chosen by Archibald MacLeish for the Yale Series of Younger Poets in 1944. A selection of his prose has been collected in *Poems Are Hard to Read*. At Princeton University in 1940, Meredith wrote his senior honors thesis on Robert Frost entitled *An Analysis of the Poetic Method of Robert Frost*, about which Frost inscribed, in a copy now in the Shain Library at Connecticut College, the following note: "My gratitude to the author for taking all the pains over work of mine and not wishing on my evaluation of his results. I am assured on the best authority his results are very good. No man is supposed to look at himself in the glass except to shave."

Gary Metras is the author of *Until There Is Nothing Left*, a collection of poems. He is editor and printer of Adastra Press, specializing in handcrafted letterpress chapbooks. He lives in Easthampton, Massachusetts.

Thylias Moss is the author of a book for children, a memoir, and seven collections of poetry, most recently *Slave Moth*, a narrative in verse, and *Last Chance for the Tarzan Holler*, a finalist for the 1998 National Book Critics Circle Award. She teaches at the University of Michigan.

Howard Nemerov was born in 1920 in New York. He taught at Washington University where he was Distinguished Poet-in-Residence from 1969 until his death in 1991. Nemerov's many collections of poems include *Trying Conclusions: New and Selected Poems, 1961–1991* and *The Collected Poems of Howard Nemerov*, which won the Pulitzer Prize and the National Book Award in 1978. He received the Bollingen Prize in 1981. His novels include *The Homecoming Game*; *Federigo: or the Power of Love*; and *The Melodramatists*. He served as poetry consultant to the Library of Congress in 1963 and 1964, and as poet laureate of the United States from 1988 to 1990.

William Olsen is the author of of three collections of poems, *The Hand of God and a Few Bright Flowers*, *Vision of a Storm Cloud*, and *Trouble Lights*. He coedited *Planet on the Table: Poets on the Reading Life*. He teaches in the creative writing programs at Western Michigan University and Vermont College.

Ron Overton teaches at SUNY–Stony Brook in the Program in Writing and Rhetoric. His collections of poems include *Psychic Killed by Train, Hotel Me, Love on the Alexander Hamilton*, and *Dead Reckoning*.

Jay Parini is a prolific anthologist, editor, poet, novelist, cultural critic, essayist, and biographer. His novels include *Patch Boys, Benjamin's Crossing, The Apprentice Lover,* and *The Last Station: A Novel of Tolstoy's Last Year*; his collections of poetry include *Anthracite Country, House of Days: Poems*, and *Town Life*; and his biographies include *Robert Frost: A Life, John Steinbeck: A Biography*, and *One Matchless Time: A Life of William Faulkner*. He is editor of *The Oxford Encyclopedia of American Literature, The Columbia Anthology of American Poetry, The Norton Book of American Biography*, and *American Identities: Contemporary Multicultural Voices*. He is on the faculty of Middlebury College in Vermont.

Linda Pastan's most recent collection of poems is *The Last Uncle*. Other collections include *Carnival Evening: New and Selected Poems 1968–1998*, a finalist for the National Book Award; *An Early Afterlife; Heroes in Disguise; The Imperfect Paradise; PM/AM: New and Selected Poems; The Five Stages of Grief*; and *A Perfect Circle of Sun*. In 1993, she recieved the Ruth Lilly Poetry Prize. From 1991 to 1994, she served as the poet laureate of Maryland. She lives in Potomac, Maryland.

Joyce Peseroff is the author of three collections of poems: *The Hardness Scale, A Dog in the Lifeboat*, and *Mortal Education*. She is editing a collection of essays on the poet Jane Kenyon. She lives in Lexington, Massachusetts.

David Ray is the author of more than ten collections of poetry, most recently *One Thousand Years: Poems about the Holocaust; Demons in the Diner; Kangaroo Paws: Poems Written in Australia*; and *The Maharani's New Wall*. He is also the author of a memoir, *The Endless Search*. The founding editor of *New Letters* magazine, Ray retired as Professor Emeritus from the University of Missouri and now lives in Tucson, Arizona, with his wife, the writer Judy Ray.

F. D. Reeve's publications include some twenty books of poetry, fiction, literary criticism, and essays. Recent collections of poems include *A World You Haven't Seen: Selected Poems; The Urban Stampede and Other*

Poems; and *The Moon and Other Failures*. In 1962, Reeve accompanied Robert Frost to Russia, serving as his translator. His account of this fascinating trip was recorded in *Robert Frost in Russia*. Originally published in 1964, *Robert Frost in Russia* was reissued in a new and updated edition in 2001. The founding editor of *Poetry Review*, Reeve retired from Wesleyan University where he was professor of Russian.

John Ridland retired from teaching in the English department at the College of Creative Studies at the University of California, Santa Barbara, in 2004. Among his several collections of poems are *Elegy for My Aunt* and *In the Shadowless Light*. From 1966–1972, he edited the *Little Square Review*. He is currently preparing a selection of Frost's poems for Hesperus Press.

Pattiann Rogers is the author of ten collections of poems, most recently *Generations* and *Song of the World Becoming, New and Collected Poems, 1981–2001*, selected as a finalist for the *L. A. Times* Book Prize. She has been the recipient of grants and awards from the National Endowment for the Arts, Guggenheim Foundation, and the Lannan Foundation. In May 2000, she was a resident at the Rockefeller Foundation's Bellagio Study and Conference Center in Bellagio, Italy.

Gibbons Ruark is the author of *Passing through Customs: New and Selected Poems*; *Forms of Retrieval*; *Rescue the Perishing*; *Keeping Company*; *Reeds*; and *A Program for Survival*. Since 1968, he has taught English at the University of Delaware. He lives in Landenberg, Pennsylvania.

Muriel Rukeyser is the author of twenty collections of poetry, among them *Theory of Flight*, which won the Yale Series of Younger Poets' Award in 1935; *Waterlily Fire: Poems 1932–1962*; *The Collected Poems of Muriel Rukeyser*; and *Out of Silence: Selected Poems*. Her collection of lecture-essays, *The Life of Poetry*, remains a standard of American poetics. She was also a novelist, a dramatist, and an anthologist. She died in 1980 in New York.

Lex Runciman's poetry collections are *Continuo*; *Out of Town*; *The Admirations*, recipient of the 1989 Oregon Book Award; and *Luck*. He directs the Writing Center at Linfield College in McMinnville, Oregon.

Lynn Veach Sadler is the author of the chapbook *Poet Geography*. Her play *Sassing the Sphinx* was commissioned for the First International Robert Frost Symposium, and "Why God Chose Robert Frost over Elvis" is adapted from her second Frost play, *Not Your Average Poet*. A former college president, she now lives in North Carolina.

Mary Jo Salter is the author of five collections of poetry, including *Unfinished Painting*, winner of the Lamont Prize; *Sunday Skaters*; and, most recently, *Open Shutters*. She is also an editor of *The Norton Anthology of Poetry*. She is currently Emily Dickinson Senior Lecturer in the Humanities at Mt. Holyoke College.

Peter Schmitt is the author of *Country Airport* and *Hazard Duty*, both from Copper Beech Press. He is the recipient of The "Discovery"/*The Nation* Prize for Poetry, the Lavan Younger Poets Award from the Academy of American Poets, and grants from the Ingram Merrill Foundation and Florida Arts Council.

Delmore Schwartz — poet, critic, short story writer, teacher — is the author of *In Dreams Begin Responsibilities and Other Stories*; *Selected Poems: Summer Knowledge*; *Successful Love and Other Stories*; *Selected Essays of Delmore Schwartz*; *Last and Lost Poems*; *The Ego Is Always at the Wheel: Bagatelles*, *Portrait of Delmore* (journals), and a selection of correspondence with James Laughlin, *Delmore Schwartz and James Laughlin: Selected Letters*. He was poetry editor at *Partisan Review* (1943–1955) and poetry and film critic at the *New Republic* (1955–1957). He taught at Harvard and Syracuse universities. He received the Bollingen Prize in Poetry in 1960. In 1960, he was invited to attend the inauguration of John F. Kennedy as President of the United States — in the company of W. H. Auden, Robert Frost, Allen Tate, and William Carlos Williams — but the invitation arrived four months late because of his many address changes. His poem "Calmly We Walk Through This April's Day" inspired the *Star Trek* movie *Star Trek: Generations*, and he was given screen credit. He died of a heart attack in 1966 at the age of 52, in New York, where his body lay unclaimed in the morgue at Bellevue Hospital even after the *New York Times* printed a lengthy obituary.

Edmund Skellings founded the University of Alaska Writers Workshop and established an MFA degree there. At Florida Atlantic University, he founded and directed the International Institute for Creative Communication. In 1990, he established the Florida Center for Electronic Communication, where he now directs and teaches in the MFA program in computer arts. He has taught in the Iowa Writers' Workshop, and his award-winning animated computer poems have appeared on television in Berlin, Tokyo, Madrid, Toronto, New York, Chicago, Miami, San Francisco, and Los Angeles. His most recent book is *Collected Poems, 1958–1998*. He has served as Florida's poet laureate since 1980.

Floyd Skloot's fourth collection of poems, *The End of Dreams*, is forthcoming in 2006. His memoir, *In the Shadow of Memory*, received the 2004 PEN Center USA Literary Award in creative nonfiction and the 2004 Independent Publishers Award in creative nonfiction and was a finalist for both the Barnes & Noble Discover Award and the PEN Award for the Art of the Essay. He lives in Amity, Oregon.

Dave Smith is the author of seventeen collections of poems, including *The Wick of Memory: New and Selected Poems 1970–2000* and *Fate's Kite: Poems 1991–1995*. He also is the author of *Onliness*, a novel, and *Southern Delights*, a collection of short stories. *Local Assays: On Contemporary American Poetry* and *The Pure Clear Word: Essays on the Poetry of James Wright* are collections of his criticism. He is Elliott Coleman Professor in the Writing Seminars at Johns Hopkins University.

Laurel Smith lives in southern Indiana where she teaches, directs the honors program at Vincennes University, and works to promote the arts and literacy in this region. She is coauthor of *Early Works by Modernist Women*.

William Jay Smith has authored or edited more than fifty collections of poetry, prose, translations, literary criticism, children's books, and edited anthologies, among them *The Cherokee Lottery* (poetry); *The World below the Window, Poems 1937–1997*; *Collected Translations*; *Laughing Time: Collected Nonsense* (light verse); *Army Brat* (memoir); and *The Streaks of the Tulips* (criticism). From 1968–1970, he served as poetry consultant to the Library of Congress. Smith was poet in residence at Williams College from 1959 to 1967, chairman of the Writing Division of the School of Arts at Columbia University from 1973 until 1975, and currently is Professor Emeritus of English at Hollins College. He makes his home between Cummington, Massachusetts, and Paris, France.

Laurence Snydal is a poet, musician, and retired teacher. His poems have appeared in many journals and anthologies, and he has written two books of nonfiction. Originally from North Dakota, he lives in San Jose, California.

John Sokol is a writer and painter living in Akron, Ohio. He is the author of *Kissing the Bees*, winner of the 1999 Redgreene Press Chapbook Competition, and *In the Summer of Cancer*, a collection of poetry. His drawings and paintings are included in many public and private collections.

J. R. Solonche, with Joan Siegal, is the author of *Peach Girl: Poems for a Chinese Daughter*. His work has appeared in many journals and on National Public Radio's "Theme and Variation." He teaches at SUNY–Orange County and lives in Blooming Grove, New York.

William Stafford published more than sixty books of poetry and prose, including *Traveling through the Dark*, winner of the National Book Award for Poetry in 1963, and *Writing the Australian Crawl*, a collection of prose and interviews on the writer's craft. Stafford taught at Lewis and Clark College in Portland, Oregon, for more than thirty years. He died in 1993. His posthumous collection, *The Way It Is: New and Selected Poems*, was published in 1998.

Timothy Steele's collections of poems include *The Color Wheel* and *Sapphics and Uncertainties: Poems 1970–1986*. His most recent book is *All the Fun's In How You Say a Thing: An Explanation of Meter and Versification*. Among his honors are a Guggenheim Fellowship, a Lavan Younger Poets Award from the Academy of American Poets, and the Robert Fitzgerald Prize for the Study of Prosody. He is a professor of English at California State University, Los Angeles.

Felix Stefanile is the author of several collections of poems, including *The Country of Absence* and *The Dance at Saint Gabriel's*. He is the recipient of the first John Ciardi Award for Lifetime Achievement in Poetry. For many years, he edited the magazine *Sparrow* and its publishing imprint Sparrow Press. He retired from teaching at Purdue University and continues to live in West Lafayette, Indiana.

Edward Thomas met Robert Frost in a London restaurant in October 1913. At the time, Thomas, thirty-six, was among the leading literary critics in England, as well as a distinguished writer in his own right of biographies, a novel, and several collections of nature and travel writing, short stories, and essays. Thomas came to Dymock in April of 1914 to visit Frost, and then returned in June and then again in August with his family for holiday. Thomas and Frost enjoyed talking and walking the Gloucestershire countryside — "botanizing walks" was Frost's term for their nature treks. In "The Sun Used to Shine" Thomas recalls this important time in both poets' lives. Frost's "The Road Not Taken" was inspired, in part, by their walks and by Thomas's frequent regrets about which direction to take when coming upon crosspaths. Their brief but intense friendship was mutually beneficial. In December of 1914, at Frost's urging, Thomas began writing poems. He enlisted in the British army in July 1915, having declined Frost's invitation to return to the U.S. with him. However, Frost and Thomas continued to correspond, sending each other poems while Thomas was stationed on the Western Front. Thomas was killed in battle on Easter Monday, April 9, 1917, at 7:36 A.M., at the age of thirty-nine, in Arras, France. In his final letter to Frost, written less than a week before he was killed, Thomas wrote that he spent ten minutes every night reading Shakespeare's tragedies and smoking his pipe, and then wished Frost and his wife "Goodnight." Frost called Thomas "the only brother I never had." Frost wrote four poems about Thomas: "The Road Not Taken," "A Soldier," "Iris by Night," and "To E.T." Thomas's first collection of poems, entitled *Poems* (published under the pseudonym Edward Eastaway) and published posthumously in July 1917, was dedicated to Robert Frost. *The Collected Poems of Edward Thomas* is available from Oxford University Press. Perhaps the best accounts of Frost and his relationship to Thomas and the Dymock poets is Linda Hart's *Once They Lived in Gloucestershire: A Dymock Poets Anthology.*

Sue Ellen Thompson is the author of three books of poetry: *This Body of Silk*, *The Wedding Boat,* and *The Leaving: New and Selected Poems.* Recipient of the Nimrod-Harman Award/Pablo Neruda Prize in Poetry in 2003, she lives in Mystic, Connecticut.

Daniel Tobin is the author of three collections of poems, including *Where the World Is Made*, cowinner of the 1998 Katherine Bakeless Nason Award. Among his numerous awards is the Robert Frost Fellowship. He is also the author of *Passage to the Center: Imagination and the Sacred in the Poetry of Seamus Heaney.* Currently he is editing *The Book of Irish American Poetry from the Eighteenth Century to the Present.* He chairs the writing, literature, and publishing department at Emerson College in Boston.

Michael Van Walleghen currently teaches creative writing at the University of Illinois. He is the author of six books of poetry, most recently *In the Black Window: Poems New and Selected.*

Mark Vinz is professor of English and teaches in the MFA program in creative writing at Minnesota State University Moorhead. He is the author of several collections of poetry, including *Late Night Calls* and, most recently, *Affinities.*

Davi Walders's most recent collection of poetry is *Gifts*, commissioned by the Milton Murray Foundation for Philanthropy. She directs the Vital Signs Poetry Project at the National Institutes of Health and its Children's Inn in Bethesda, Maryland. She lives in Chevy Chase, Maryland.

Kim Waller lives in New York City, where she is a magazine writer and editor. In 1956, as a college student, she held the Robert Frost Poetry Scholarship at the Bread Loaf School of English in Ripton, Vermont, where she met Frost. Her poem recalls that first meeting. She spent many evenings with other students in Frost's cabin on the farm, where, she says, "the later the hour, the more loquacious and inspiring he became."

Daneen Wardrop is professor of English at Western Michigan University in Kalamazoo. Her poems have appeared in numerous magazines and journals. She is the author of two books of literary criticism, including *Emily Dickinson's Gothic.*

Michael Waters is the author of seven collections of poetry, including *Parthenopi: New and Selected Poems*. He is the editor of *Contemporary American Poetry* (7th Edition) and *Perfect in Their Art: Poems on Boxing from Homer to Ali*. He teaches at Salisbury University in Maryland and for the New England College MFA Program. He is the 2005 Stadler Poet-in-Residence at Bucknell University.

Bruce Weigl is the author of ten collections of poetry, among them *The Unraveling Strangeness*; *Archeology of the Circle: New and Selected Poems*; *After the Others*; and *Song of Napalm*. He is also the author of a memoir, *The Circle of Hanh*. He currently lives in Oberlin, Ohio, and is Distinguished Visiting Professor at Lorain County Community College.

Roger Weingarten is the author of eight collections of poetry, including *Ghost Wrestling*, *Infant Bonds of Joy*, *Shadow Shadow*, and *The Vermont Suicides*. He also has edited the anthologies *New American Poets of the '90s* and *Poets of the New Century*. He founded and currently teaches in the MFA program at Vermont College. He lives in Montpelier, Vermont.

Theodore Weiss published fourteen volumes of poetry, among them *From Princeton One Autumn Afternoon: The Collected Poems of Theodore Weiss 1950–1986* and *Selected Poems*. For nearly sixty years, he and his wife Renée edited the *Quarterly Review of Literature*. In 1997, he and Renée won a PEN Club Special Lifetime Award for their editing; and Ted received the William/Derwood Prize for his poetry. At the time of his death in 2003, he and Renée were collaborating on a collection of poems. He was Professor Emeritus at Princeton University, where he taught for twenty-one years.

Gail White's collections of poems include *The Price of Everything* and *Greatest Hits*. With Katherine McAlpine, she edited the anthology *The Muse Strikes Back: A Poetic Response by Women to Men*. She lives in Breaux Bridge, Louisiana.

Richard Wilbur's books of poetry include *Collected Poems: 1943–2004*; *New and Collected Poems*, which won the 1989 Pulitzer Prize; *The Mind-Reader: New Poems*; *Walking to Sleep: New Poems and Translations*; *Advice to a Prophet and Other Poems*; *Things of This World*, for which he received the 1957 Pulitzer Prize and the National Book Award; *Ceremony and Other Poems*; and *The Beautiful Changes and Other Poems*. He has also published numerous translations of French plays, books for children, and a collection of prose. He received the Bollingen Prize in Poetry in 1971. He was elected a chevalier of the Ordre des Palmes Académiques and is a former poet laureate of the United States. A Chancellor Emeritus of the Academy of American Poets, he lives in Cummington, Massachusetts.

Steve Wilson is the author of *Allegory Dance* and *The Singapore Express*. He teaches at Texas State University in San Marcos and has been a Fulbright Lecturer in Romania and Slovenia.

Permissions

We are grateful to the authors, editors, and publishers who have given us permission to reprint poems.

Joe Aimone, "A Second-Grade Incident from Robert Frost's Childhood," first appeared in the *Formalist* 6, issue 1, 1995. Copyright © 1995 by Joe Aimone. Reprinted by permission of the author.

Tony Barnstone, "Trying to Sleep on My Father's Couch and Staring at the Fractured Plaster, I Recall." Copyright © 2003 by Tony Barnstone. Reprinted by permission of the author.

Willis Barnstone, "Late December, Where Are You, Robert Frost?" From *The Secret Reader: 501 Sonnets*, University Press of New England, 1996. Copyright © 1996 by Willis Barnstone. Reprinted by permission of the author.

Marvin Bell, "Unable to Sleep in Frost's Bed in Franconia." Copyright © 2004 by Marvin Bell. Reprinted by permission of the author.

Wendell Berry, "Stay Home." From *The Selected Poems of Wendell Berry*, Counterpoint Press, 1998. Copyright © 1999 by Wendell Berry. Reprinted by permission of Perseus Books Group and the author.

Robert Bly, "Frost and His Enemies." Copyright © 2004 by Robert Bly. Reprinted by permission of the author.

Alec Bond, "After Snow-Mobiling." From *North of Sioux Falls*. Spoon River Poetry Press, 1983. Copyright © 1983 by Alec Bond. Reprinted by permission of the publisher.

N. M. Brewka, "Elinor White Frost Speaks." Copyright © 2004 by N. M. Brewka. Reprinted by permission of the author.

Kim Bridgford, "Robert Frost" first appeared in the *Formalist* 13, issue 2, 2002. Copyright © 2002 by Kim Bridgford. Reprinted by permission of the author.

Gwendolyn Brooks, "Of Robert Frost." From *Selected Poems of Gwendolyn Brooks*. Copyright © 1999 by Gwendolyn Brooks. Reprinted by consent of Brooks Permissions.

Index